Stephen Penton

The Guardian's Instruction

The Gentleman's Romance

Stephen Penton

The Guardian's Instruction
The Gentleman's Romance

ISBN/EAN: 9783744693547

Printed in Europe, USA, Canada, Australia, Japan

Cover: Foto ©Thomas Meinert / pixelio.de

More available books at **www.hansebooks.com**

HE GUARDIAN'S INSTRUCTION

OR

THE GENTLEMAN'S ROMANCE

WRITTEN FOR THE DIVERSION AND SERVICE

OF THE GENTRY ((/

BY STEPHEN PENTON

REPRINTED FROM THE EDITION OF 1688

WITH AN INTRODUCTION BY HERBERT H. STURMER

LONDON

F. E. ROBINSON

20 GREAT RUSSELL STREET

1897

INTRODUCTION.

I. 'THE GUARDIAN'S INSTRUCTION.'

THE Guardian's Instruction is ranked by bibliographers as a scarce book; indeed, it is possible that not many book-lovers of the present day have handled a copy of it. Even the Lambeth Palace Library, that stately and peaceful home of so many seventeenth-century volumes, the shrine of an example of at least one tiny book (of the time of Charles the Second) which I hardly hope to encounter elsewhere, has no copy of ' The Guardian's Instruction.' The present edition of that little treatise is reprinted from a copy of the book which is now in the possession of Mr. F. E. Robinson.

The Guardian's Instruction is of interest for the following (and other) reasons : I. For the opinions which it sets forth upon educational matters, such as the home-training (*e.g.*, pp. 68-9) and subsequent schooling (*e.g.*, p. 31), of the sons of persons of position, and the tuition of undergraduates at Oxford. II. Because it contains (*e.g.*, pp. 17-18, 40-44, 51, 73-74, 76) much first-hand information as to the detail of University life at Oxford at various seventeenth-century dates. III. For its allusions to political and social questions or events (*e.g.*, pp. 15-16, 19, 23, 53, 57, 59, 61, 64, 75). IV. For the witty garb in which its teaching appeals to the reader. V. Because it was written by an Oxford don (and Anglican clergyman) of a charming type, by a man who was 'a scholar and a gentleman' in a very strict sense of that somewhat hackneyed phrase.

As will be seen upon the title-page of the reprint, *The Guardian's Instruction* did not appear in print until 1688, and it was then an entirely anonymous publication. Judging by internal evidence, much of the book may have been, part of it must have been, written during the last four years of the reign of Charles the Second. I have hunted up a contemporary mention of its *publication*, which took place in ('Hillary-Term 168⅞,' that is, in) *January* 168⅞.

This notice runs thus: 'The Guardian's Instructions (*sic*), shewing the Necessity, and also the Method of a stricter Education of the Children of the Nobility and Gentry, in order to their living happily and usefully in all Conditions of Life. Twelves. Price bound 1s. Sold by *S. Miller* at the Star near the West end of St. *Pauls.*'

In 1694 there was published a book, of a not very dissimilar kind, entitled, 'New Instructions to the Guardian: shewing That the last Remedy to Prevent the Ruin,

Advance the Interest, and Recover the Honour of this Nation is, I. A more Serious and Strict Education of the Nobility and Gentry. II. To breed up all their younger Sons to some calling and Employment. III. More of them to Holy Orders. With a Method of Institution (*sic*) from Three Years of Age, to Twenty One. . . . London. . . . 1694.' This book appeared in 'Trinity-Term 1694,' according to a contemporary mention of it.

After the title-page leaf of 'New Instructions to the Guardian' there comes an 'Epistle Dedicatory' addressed 'To Charles[1] Lord Bruce, Son[2] and Heir to the Right Honourable the Earl of Ailesbury.' This preface begins thus : ' My Lord, I am very willing it should be known how great a share of the *Guardian's Instruction* was Influenc'd by the Prospect of your good Lordship's Education ; and also the just Regard these Second Thoughts have both to your Lordship, and the Splendid Families of *Saresden, Barton,* and *Glympton.*' It ends with the signature of '. . . Your most Obliged, and Affectionate, STEPHEN PENTON.'

[1] Succeeded his father Thomas as third *Earl of Ailesbury* (first creation of 166¾) in November 1741. Charles seems to have been born between 1680—6.
[2] Second but only surviving son.

II. THE AUTHOR.

A certain Mr. Stephen Penton was therefore the author of *The Guardian's Instruction.* And who was the said Mr. Penton? Well, thanks to the treasuries of information about Oxford matters of a byegone age which were formed for posterity by such writers as Anthony Wood and Thomas Hearne, and thanks also to the clues to details about Stephen Penton collected in our own day by the Rev. J. T. Fowler, Mr. W. P. Courtney, and others, I need give way but little to the genealogist's liking for hunting up facts about noteworthy people in answering that question. Indeed, the Oxonian reader will not echo such a question at all, for Stephen Penton, scarce and forgotten as the products of his literary activity have become, was a well-known figure in the Oxford of Charles the Second's time, having been a Fellow of New College from 1661 to 1672, and Principal of St. Edmund Hall from February 167$\frac{5}{8}$ to March 168$\frac{3}{4}$.

Nevertheless, it is quite possible that there may be readers who will prefer that a new edition of Penton's quaint little treatise should be prefaced by a short sketch of his life. Therefore, although with some diffidence, I venture to print the following paragraphs, in which the quotation marks (where not otherwise explained) refer to one or other of the writings of Anthony Wood. The names of the other authors to whom I have been indebted for facts are mostly given in footnotes. In all such cases I quote from an author directly, and in many instances I have checked my printed page by his.

STEPHEN PENTON was born March 30, 1639, in the parish[1] of St. John's ' in the city of Winchester,' and was baptised[2] at St. John's Church, April 9, 1639. He was a son of Stephen Penton of Winchester.[3] His armorial bearings were 'per chevron gules and or, in chief two castles ar., in base a lion rampant az.'[4] Thus it is evident that our author was a member of the Penton family which (in the eighteenth century) furnished members of Parliament for Winchester.[5] Stephen Penton was 'educated in grammar learning in Wykeham's school,' having been duly elected to the foundation of that famous seat of English education. He was admitted in 1653.[1] From Winchester College he went up with a scholarship to New College, Oxford, whence he matriculated on June 28, 1659.[6] Before the end of that year he was ' elected prob.[ationary] fellow' of his college.

[1] T. F. Kirby : *Winchester Scholars.*
[2] Rev. J. T. Fowler : *Memorials of Ripon,* ii. (1886).
[3] W. P. Courtney : article in *D.N.B.*
[4] Nichols : *The Topographer and Genealogist,* 1858.
[5] See pages xxv-vi of this ' Introduction.'
[6] Joseph Foster : *Alumni Oxonienses* (early series), vol. iii.

In 1661 he became a full Fellow,[1] and graduated[2] B.A. on May 5, 1663, and M.A. on January 17, 166⅘. Nearly all my authorities speak of him as afterward B.D., but I have found no printed record of the date of the degree. In 1665 the 'same day the king came in, viz., M., Sept. the 25, the Spanish embassadour, count de Molena, came to New Coll., which was appointed for his lodging; and being meet by the warden [Michael Woodward] and fellows at the gate, Mr. [Stephen] Penton spoke a Latine speech to him; which done the Spanish embassadour answered him in Spanish, which was interpreted in English to them.'[3] In 1670 Penton 'had the rectory of Tingewick in Bucks conferr'd on him by the warden and society of his coll.' Tingewick is two miles west of Buckingham railway station. In or before 1671 he was appointed a chaplain to Robert,[4] Earl of Ailesbury and Elgin, who was himself a scholar and an antiquary, as well as a lover of learning in others; at some date Penton acted as tutor to a member of the Bruce family. A modern authority appears to be

[1] Kirby : *Winchester Scholars.*
[2] *Catalogue of . . . Graduates . . . of Oxford.* Oxford, 1851 : this has ' 1666' which my text (following Mr. Foster) gives as ' 166⅘,' not as 166⅚.
[3] Rev. Andrew Clark : *Life and Times of Anthony Wood . . . described by himself.* (Oxford Hist. Society) 1891-5.
[4] The first Earl of Ailesbury : died 1685.

convinced that the pupil was Thomas, Lord Bruce (see note 4 page xiii), and Wood's statement may be only an attempt to say the same thing, but it reads as if the pupil were Charles[1] Bruce. I have compared all the dates and facts that I could obtain as to this point, without becoming satisfied to speak decisively about it here. Penton appears to have vacated his fellowship of New in 1672.[2]

Stephen Penton was elected Principal of St. Edmund Hall 'by the Provost and Fellows of Queen's College, Feb. 15,' 167⅝ (and 'admitted by the Vice-Chancellor the 17th of the said month') on condition 'that he resign the Rectory of Tingwicke in com. Bucks, and that the Society of New College present a Fellow of Queen's College thereunto.' On March 26, 1679, he obtained over ninety votes as a (defeated) candidate for the office of public orator; it seems that he was 'a good orator.'[3] On July 7, 1682, he preached the 'Latin Sermon.'[4] As Principal of St. Edmund Hall, Penton made himself of use to those about him, in accordance with his habit. 'The first stone of the Chapel was laid on Monday, Apr. 19, 1680'; it was consecrated April 7, 1682.

---

[1] Charles, Lord Bruce, became third Earl of Ailesbury in 1741 (G. E. C.: *Complete Peerage of England, etc.*)

[2] Kirby : *Winchester Scholars.*

[3] Wood : (edit. Andrew Clark, and elsewhere).

[4] Rev. J. T. Fowler : *Memorials of Ripon.*

'It stands at the east end of the Court,' and was erected, together with the Library, at the charge of Stephen Penton (with some little help from acquaintances of his, such as Bishop Prichett of Gloucester, Sir Jonathan Raymond, and 'Counsellor' Keck).[1] 'Over the Chapel door is this memorial engraven on a tablet :

DEO OPT. MAX.
Capellam hanc sumtu
Suo et Amicorum posuit
STEPHANUS PENTON, S.T.B.
Istius Aulæ Principalis.
Anno Domini MDCLXXXII.'[1]

Hearne[2] says that this inscription was written and put up by Dr. John Mill, Penton's successor (after the interval of Crosthwaite's brief rule) in the principalship. From the same informant comes a story[3] of the (characteristic) care with which Stephen Penton entered the names of all benefactors to St. Edmund Hall in a great vellum-bound book.

On March 7, 168¾ Penton 'resign'd up his principality of Edmund hall into the hands of the vicechancellor, who sent the resignation that morning to Queen's Coll.' : this resignation was 'for health sake.' Hearne[3] has left us a 'Memorandum also yᵗ when

[1] Gutch, additions to Wood : 1786 edition of *Hist. Coll. Oxford.*

[2] 'Notæ et Spicilegium ' to his edition of *Gulielmus Neubrigensis,* 1719, vol. iii.

[3] *Remarks and Collections* (edit. C. E. Doble, 1885-9).

M^r. Penton resign'd his Principality of Edm. Hall he bought twelve Knives and forks, the Handles silver, wch are now in the Principal's Lodgings with a silver [*sic*] and a Cover to it, all wch it seems he left for ye use of ye Principals successively.'

Stephen Penton became 'rector of Glimpton' in Oxfordshire in the summer of 1684, on the presentation of Frances Wheate,[1] widow[2] of Thomas Wheate of Glympton. (She was a daughter of Sir Robert Jenkinson, Kt., of Walcot, Oxfordshire. I find that her only son Thomas Wheate, of Glympton, M.P. for 'New' Woodstock, was created a baronet in 1696. The Wheates were related to the Thorolds of Lincolnshire and to the Quineys of Stratford-upon-Avon.[3]) Either before (as Wood seems to state) or during Penton's residence at Glympton he acted as 'lecturer' in the parish church of Churchill. (Glympton is four miles north-north-west of Blenheim-and-Woodstock railway-station, and Churchill is near ChippingNorton.)

In 1693 Penton became rector of Wath (near Ripon) 'in Yorkshire by the gift of the earl of Aylesbury[4] : whereupon he left Glimp-

---

[1] Information from deeds, etc., which are in private hands.

[2] I have not the date of her husband's death, but it is known that she became a widow at some date before 1694. Thomas Wheate presented a John Robinson to the living in 1662.

[3] Information from various printed sources.

[4] Thomas, second Earl of Ailesbury (first creation

ton about Christmas an. 1693.' (He had been instituted to the benefice of Wath on Sept. 27.)[1] On May 28, 1701, Penton became a Prebendary of Ripon by collation to the third prebendal stall.[2]

In 1702 'a considerable number of printed books were given by Steph. Penton, B.D.' to the Bodleian Library.[3] He may have visited his beloved Oxford occasionally from distant Wath, but it was evidently Henry Penton, not Stephen Penton (as has been sometimes stated), who is recorded as having preached there (in St. Mary's on September 23, 1705) a memorable sermon in which the Duke of Marlborough was praised.

In 1706 the busy brain and generous heart

---

of 166¾), and third Earl of Elgin, was born in 1656, succeeded his father in 1685, and died in 1741. [He was son of the first Earl by his wife Diana, who was second daughter of Henry (Grey) first Earl of Stamford, by his Countess Anne (heiress of Stamford) youngest daughter and co-heir of William (Cecil) second Earl of Exeter.] He married (1) Lady Elizabeth Seymour, by whom he had a son and successor, and other children (2) Charlotte D'Argentau *suo jure* Countess d'Esseneux and Baroness de Melsbroeck. He was imprisoned in 169⅚ upon an accusation of having conspired in 1695 to plan the restoration of James the Second. His first wife died in 169⅞ of terror as to what might be the earl's ultimate fate. See G. E. C.: *Complete Peerage of England, etc.*: Macaulay's *History*.

[1] Nichols : *The Topographer and Genealogist.*
[2] Fowler : *Mem. of Ripon.*
[3] Rev. W. Dunn Macray : *Annals of the Bodleian Library.* 2nd ed. 1890.

of Penton failed his parishioners for the first
time, for their rector passed away on
October 17 in that year, and his body was
buried[1] in the chancel[2] of Wath church on
October 20.

Hearne[3] says that the following epitaph,
which is inscribed upon a brass plate in the
chancel of Wath church, was composed by
Stephen Penton himself. I quote it here,
however, from a copy most kindly given to
me by the present (1897) Rector of Wath[4]
(the Rev. H. R. Hunter), as Hearne's (doubtless second- or third-hand) form of it contains slight inaccuracies :

   [A SMALL REPRESENTATION OF]
   [ARMORIAL BEARINGS.]
HEAR LIES WHAT'S LEFT OF STEPHEN PENTOn
RECTOR WHO BEING DEAD YET SPEAKETH ONCE
FOR ALL ≋ MY BELOVED PARISHIONERS ≋ ----
SINCE ANY ONE OF YOV MAY BE THE NEXT----
LET EVERY ONE PREPARE TO BE SO ---- MENT
TO PREPARE FOR DEATH DEVOVTLY RECEIVE THE SACRA
TO PREPARE AGAINST SVDDEN DEATH RECEIVE IT ---
OFTEN≋MAKE YOVR WILL WHILE YOV ARe IN GOOD HEALTH
THAT YOV MAY HAVE LEISVRE TO DIE WISELY ----
AND IF YOV HOPE TO DIE COMFORTABLY -----
YOV MVST RESOLVE TO LIVE RIGTEOVSLY ---
≋ GOD SEND VS ALL AN HAPPY MEETING ≋
HE WAS BORNE AT WINCHESTER WAS FORMERLY FELLOW
OF NEW COLLEDGE PRINCIPAL OF EDMVNDS HALL ----
AND RECTOR OF GLIMPTON ALL IN OXON AND ALSO --
----- RECTOR OF TINGSWICK IN BVCKS -----
HE DIED RECTOR OF THIS CHVRCH OF WATH
 AND PREBENDARIE OF RIPON OCTOBER 18TH
  ANNO DMI 1706 ETAT SVÆ 67

---

[1] Nichols : quoting *parish register.*
[2] Fowler : *Mem. of Ripon.*
[3] 'Notæ et Spicilegium' in his edition of *Gulielmus
Neubrigensis.*
[4] The benefice of Wath is now in the gift of a Mar-

The true verdict as to Stephen Penton's character is doubtless the one left to us[1] by Thomas Hearne (a veracious writer[2]) in the following words : ' Mr. Stephen Penton . . . was an ingenious, honest Man, a good Scholar, a quaint Preacher, of a most facetious Temper, of extraordinary good Nature (which made him belov'd by all People ; for, I think, I never heard anyone speak ill of him), a despiser of Money and Preferments (for he might have been advanced as he pleased) . . .' In an old MS. volume which belongs to the parish of Wath, Stephen Penton is spoken of as ' The very Reverend Learned and Pious M[r.] Stephen Penton.'

The following extracts, which I take from the Rev. Stephen Penton's holograph will[3] (dated October 8, 1706), go far to confirm Hearne's words :

' Interceede, blessed Lord and Saviour, at God's right hand for all the sins it [my Spirit] hath been tempted to by an ill habit

---

quis, as it was in Penton's day in the gift of an Earl, of Ailesbury.

[1] In the ' Notæ et Spicilegium ' from which I have quoted before. Elsewhere Hearne says of Stephen Penton : 'he always declin'd Greatness, being a truly Honest, good Man, & an Excell[t] Scholar, & of so good & facetious a temper (without Reserve) y[t] he was belov'd by all that knew him. He has written . . . two little things in 8° about y[e] *Guardian's Duty.*'

[2] According to Philip Bliss.

[3] As printed by Rev. J. T. Fowler.

and constitucion of body: for all the many failings of dutye, in the severall conditions of my life, & the various relations I have borne to others. Oh my gratious Redeemer, interceed most especially for all the many failings & omissions in my calling, accept of my repentance and forgive me that ever I undertook the great charge of the most holy profession.

'As for my body that my living & dying may be all of a peece I earnestly desire to be buryed with the greatest privacy and cheapness that can be ; and because I know not how to gett good wine I leave nothing to be dranck at my funerall . . . the poore [are to be invited] to a good dole of bread: the poore in my rectory I give also a dole of five pounds to be distributed after my funerall according to the degrees of their poverty & want . . .

As for library my best bookes were disposed of when the chappell was built. . . . Lastly my will is that after all necessary charges and legacies are discharged (for debts I thank God I owe none but good will to mankind & thanks to all my friends) the summe that shall remaine upon an account to be showen to the minister for the time being & over-seers, that summ I give for the use of the poore belonging to the rectorye' [viz. parish][1] to pay for nursing, surgery, etc.

[1] Nichols tells us that in 1719 the proceeds of this bequest were applied to the purchase of a small estate at Sharow near Ripon.

III. Stephen Penton's Writings.

I do not find that any of Stephen Penton's books have been reprinted since his death. The following account of them is as full a one as I have so far been able to get together.

(1) Hearne[1] says 'There is in D.r Charlett's Study amongst his Miscellanies, Num. 52. a little Book 8.vo. conc. y.e Table & Altar at y.e Beginning of which there is a Memorand. y.t the Author was M.r. Penton. The Memorand. by D.r. Charlett, I think.' Wood refers to this, more explicitly, as '*A Discourse concerning the Worship of God towards the holy Table or Altar.* Lond. 1682. in 9 sh. in oct.' I have not been able to identify this book.

(2) *The Guardian's Instruction . . . . 1688.* [For the full title of this book the reader may be referred to the title-page of the reprint which follows this 'Introduction.'] Mr. F. E. Robinson's copy is an 8vo., and consists of: Imprimatur-page-leaf, title-page-leaf, twelve pages of preface; a text, the pages of which are numbered 1-90; and two pages of index.

Under the 'Imprimatur' which is printed opposite the title-page of *New Instructions to the Guardian . . . . 1694,* I notice the following 'Advertisement': 'The Pages of the

---

[1] *Remarks and Collections.*

Introduction. xix

Guardian's Instruction, and the *Apparatus ad Theologiam,* which are so often referred to in this Book, are according to the first and best Impression, sold by *Walter Kettilby,* and *Sam. Smith* in St. *Paul*'s Church-yard. and *Henry Clements* in *Oxford.*'

I find no modern, and no other seventeenth-century, reference to the existence of more than one 'impression' of 'The Guardian's Instruction.' However, on comparing Mr. F. E. Robinson's copy (A) of the book with the only other copy (a) to which I have access, I *do* find differences in them—variations which are chiefly unimportant differences of commas, or occasional slight alterations in the spelling of a word, and so forth. Only half-a-dozen or so of these differences are so large as to be additions subtractions or variations of a few words. These can hardly be said to affect the text appreciably, as they have the air of being lesser ' author's corrections,' so that I must not discuss here the points which this little discovery suggests as to the history of this one - edition - in - more - than - one - impression book. Suffice it to say that the two impressions which I have compared can be distinguished by noticing the fact that (A) reads 'vye,' whereas (a) reads 'Vye,' in the first page of the preface. If that page is imperfect in any copy of the book which one is examining, it may be useful to remember that the heading ' The Guardian's Instruction ' on page ɪ of the text is printed in capitals in (a) but is printed in (A) in the same style in which it is given in the modern reprint of ' The Guardian's Instruction ' which follows this ' Introduction.' Whichever ' impression ' we consider to be slightly the better has many of the errors which the other one shews, so that the expression ' best,' if it was applied to either, was somewhat hypercritical.

(3) *Apparatus ad Theologiam, in usum Academiarum. I. Generalis. II. Specialis. Autore Stephano Penton, Rectore de Glympton. Oxon. Londini . . . . . 1688.* This is an 8vo. volume. On looking through it I find that it contains : Imprimatur - page - leaf, title-page-leaf, seven unnumbered pages of ' Epistola Dedicatoria ' a blank page, eleven unnumbered pages of ' Præfatio,' a blank page ; a text, the pages of which are numbered 1-157, and a blank page ; five Indices and a blank page, which, with a ' Bibliotheca Theologica Minor ' bibliography and an ' errata ' ¡page, make thirty-eight pages more. The text contains : *A. Generalis* pp. 1-[52] (including a blank page at the end), *A. Specialis* pp. 53-157 (including a blank page at the end of three of its four parts).

The ' Epistola Dedicatoria ' is inscribed ' Illustrissimo Domino Domino Thomæ Comiti de Alesbury & Elgin . . . . .' The ' Præfatio ' is ' Præfatio ad Juniores Academicos, præsertim Socios Novi Collegii Oxon.'

Some copies of the Apparatus ad Theologiam were printed upon large paper. Examples of this form of the book are said to be extremely rare.

(4) *New Instructions to the Guardian* . . . . *1694.*[1] An 8vo. The copy which I have looked through consists of: Imprimatur-page-leaf (the Imprimatur is that of 'Geo. Royse' and the date 'March 6. 169¾') title-page-leaf, seven pages of *The Epistle Dedicatory*, a blank page, eight pages of 'Contents'; a text, the pages of which are numbered 1-143; and a blank page. The text is divided into: a first part (pp. 1-[40] including a blank page) headed on page 1 'A Word to the Wise,' a second part (pp. [41]-120) beginning with a title-page of its own, a third part (pp. [121]-143) beginning with a title-page of its own.

(5) Dr. Samuel Knight, Prebendary of Ely, in his *Life of Dr. John Colet* (edition 1724, page 145) says: 'We have a late Instance of the like humble Condescension in the Head of a Hall [note, *Mr.* Stephen Penton, *Principal of S.* Edmund Hall, Oxon.] at *Oxford;* a very worthy and noted Man, who not only publish'd *The Guardian's Instruction for Youth*, but (even laterly) a *Hornbook* (or A, B, C.) for Children.'

Supposing Dr. Knight to mean this statement in its literal sense, a hornbook can hardly be ranked as one of Stephen Penton's writings. May it not be, however, a jocular

[1] See page vi of this ' Introduction.'

allusion to some production rather more booklike than a hornbook, even perhaps to such a thing as is now called a 'first reader' for children? If so, I have not succeeded in finding a copy of it, or even a useful allusion to it ; although several books of this kind did appear during Penton's lifetime. (Any reader who is curious about hornbooks may like me to mention here Mr. Andrew Tuer's *History of the Hornbook,* a most entertaining work.)

IV. STEPHEN PENTON'S RELATIVES.

The will[1] of the Rev. Stephen Penton, Rector of Wath, mentions the following relatives :

(1) 'my brother Henry Penton of Lincolne Inn.'

(2) 'my nephew John Penton and his wife.'

(3) ' my neece Barnaby & her husband.'

(4) ' my nephew Harry Penton of New Coll.'

(5) ' my nephew Thomas Penton.'

Concerning (1) I have found no information. The persons numbered (2) may be the parents of (7) Henry Penton [see below]. As for (3), the will mentions a 'Mr. Barnaby rector of Wolverton ' — probably Gabriel Barnaby of New College, Oxford (a Proctor

---

[1] Fowler : *Memorials of Ripon.*

in 1694), sometime Rector of Weeke (or Wyke) near Winchester.

With regard to (4) Henry Penton, *Winchester Scholars* says that he was born in the parish of St. Lawrence, Winchester. He was a son of Godson Penton of Winchester, matriculated from New College, Oxford, on August 11, 1684, took his M.A. degree in January, 169½, and was Vicar of Andover, Hants, in 1712.[1] From Mr. Kirby's *Winchester Scholars* we learn that Henry Penton became a scholar of Winchester College in 1680, and that he was afterwards a scholar of New College, Oxford. He held a fellowship of New College from '1683 to 1709,' and in 1708 was admitted to a fellowship of Winchester College. He bequeathed £400 to Winchester College and £100 to New College. It was evidently he who preached the sermon (at St. Mary's, Oxford, Sept. 23, 1705) which has been sometimes credited to Stephen Penton, a sermon containing an encomium of the Duke of Marlborough. In looking for Penton facts in some volumes of *The Genealogist* I have found the following entry from the *burial* register of St. James's, Bath: '1728 June 10 The Reverend M[r]. Harry Penton.'

Hearne[2] says [entry under date October 25, 1707]: 'M[r]. Penton, Nephew to M[r]. Stephen Penton, Fellow of New Coll., has bought D[r]. Mill's Study of Books for about

---

[1] Foster: *Alumni Oxonienses.*
[2] *Remarks and Collections.*

two hundred libs.' Elsewhere Hearne speaks
of ' Mᵣ. Penton of New Coll.' as the possessor
of a rare old book.

Concerning (5) I find nothing.

The Rev. Stephen Penton of Wath had
another nephew, named Stephen Penton (6),
not mentioned in the will. He may have
died before its date. He was a Winchester
scholar, took his M.A. degree from St.
Edmund Hall in 1684, and (says Mr. Joseph
Foster) was ' perhaps' the Stephen Penton
who was ' rector of Shepton Beauchamp,
Somerset, 1688-92, of Glympton, Oxon,
1693-1732, and vicar of St. Bartholomew-
the-Less, London, 1697-1700.' I doubt the
' Glympton . . . 1693.'

Wood has the following anecdote of this son
of Godson Penton. (The reference is to the fes-
tivities which took place at Oxford in honour
of the accession of James II. in February,
168⅘.) 'The same night . . . [there was]
. . . a larg bonfier before Allsoules College
gate, where the drummers beat, as they did
at most fiers. Mr. Stephen Penton, M.A. of S.
Edmund Hall (nephew to the late principall)
did bring there the bill of exclusion of James
duke of York, and telling the societie what
it was, they first tore it in pieces and then
committed it to the flames.' The same
authority tells us that this Penton was a
(defeated) candidate 'for Camden's pro-
fessorship' in November, 1691.

The following persons were evidently

members of the family to which Stephen Penton belonged.

(7) Henry Penton, son of John Penton, born in the parish[1] of St. Laurence, Winchester. His age was sixteen when he matriculated[1] from New College, Oxford, January 31, 172½. He was elected M.P. for the borough of Tregony[2] in Cornwall May 1, 1734, and sat for it until 1747. He was M.P. for Winchester[2] from July 2, 1747, until 1761. Oldfield says : ' In 1747, Henry Penton, esq., of this city, overcame the Bolton interest ; and that gentleman and the late Duke of Chandos nominated each a member during their lives.' Henry Penton was married, and had children.[3] In 1743 he was granted[4] the reversion of the office of ' Court-post,' and in 174⁶⁄₇ he accordingly became[5] ' Carrier of all his majesty's letters and dispatches between his court and place of residence, and the first passage or post-office,' a post worth £600 per annum. This Henry Penton died September 1, 1762.[6] His widow died May 24, 1782.[7]

(8) About Feb., 173⅔ a 'Wm. Penton[8], of Winchester, Esq.,' married a Miss Symonds,

[1] Foster : *Alumni Oxonienses.*
[2] *Parliamentary Return.*
[3] *Gent. Mag.*, vol 9 (660), and vol. 15 (614).
[4] *Ibid.*, vol. 13 (275).
[5] *Ibid.*, vol. 17 (103).
[6] *Ibid.*, vol. 32 (448).
[7] *Ibid.*, vol. 52 (263).
[8] *Ibid..*, vol. 3 (100) : ' William ' may be an error.

daughter to the wife of John Goddard, Esq.
(M.P. for Tregony, and one of the ' Commis-
saries for accomodating the Differences with
Spain ').

(9) ' Henry Penton, the younger, esq.,'
son of Henry Penton (7), was elected M.P.
for Winchester March 30, 1761, and represented the city until 1796.[1] He married in
January, 1765, a Miss Knowler,[2] a daughter
of John Knowler, Recorder of Canterbury.
(Her[3] sister Mary Knowler married the
seventh Lord Digby of Geashill, first Earl
Digby, and became mother of the second
Earl.[4]) Mrs. Penton died in April, 1808.[3]
In 1765 Penton's sister married ' Robert
Hankey, Esq. ; son of Sir Thomas.'[5] This
Henry Penton was a Lord of the Admiralty
from 1774 to 1782. He died on January 15,
1812, in Wimpole Street.[6] It seems that
this Henry Penton had a son who is still
represented in name and in blood, but to con-
tinue these genealogical jottings any further
is perhaps to wander too far away from
Stephen Penton, author of *The Guardian's
Instruction.*

[1] Various entries in *Parliamentary Return*, and in
Beatson's *Register.*
[2] *Gent. Mag.*, vol. 35 (97) : The name is given as
' Knowles ' by a clerical or printer's error.
[3] *Ibid.*, vol. 78 (372).
[4] G. E. C. : *Complete Peerage of England*, etc.
vol. iii. (1890), page 121.
[5] *Gent. Mag.*, vol. 35 (146).
[6] *Ibid.*, vol. 82 (93).

V. This Volume.

To such readers as a reprint of *The Guardian's Instruction* is likely to attract, it would be presumptuous of me to offer notes of a glossarial or historical type upon its text. Nor, indeed, do I observe any difficulties in the book which can puzzle anyone who has at hand a good *History of England* (*e.g.* Bright's, vol. ii.), and a good English dictionary (*e.g. The Encyclopædic Dictionary*) which gives the seventeenth-century meanings of words which have changed their sense or become obsolete. (How it would have delighted Stephen Penton to foresee the *New English Dictionary* which Oxford is gradually giving to the world !)

Suffice it, therefore, for me to add that the text of this (1897) edition is the exact text of the old volume (1688) from which it has been reprinted. Indeed, in spite of the substitution of the modern form of the letter ' s ' for the old forms which many eyes dislike, and some difference of paging, this edition is almost nearer akin to a ' facsimile reproduction' than to an ordinary reprint, although it does not claim to be more than the latter.

H. H. S.

October 25, 1897.

[Reprint. 1897.]

This may be printed.

Nov. 17.
1687.

Rob. Midgley.

THE
GUARDIAN'S
INSTRUCTION,
OR,
The Gentleman's Romance.

Written for
The *Diverſion* and *Service* of
THE GENTRY.

—Delectando, paritérque Monendo.

LONDON,

Printed for the Authour, and ſold by *Simon
Miller*, at the *Star* near the Weſt-end
of St. *Paul*'s, 1688.

TO THE
ENGLISH
GENTRY.

*A*Fter the very copious *Treatise of Educa-*
tion, the Gentleman's Calling, *and*
other Excellent Advices of Manners,
Civil prudence *and* Institution, *it looks*
somewhat Assuming to invade any the least
part of that Subject.

But I am so far from pretending to vye
Art and Contrivance, that the main Design
of that Part of this Tract which interferes
is to exemplifie *and illustrate the Practic-*
ableness of those General Rules and Instruc-
tions which the forementioned Authours
have deduced from Nature and Reason.
And therefore sometimes a Coincidence *of*
the same Thoughts upon the same Subject is
unavoidable, as Mr. Osborn *hath alledged*
to excuse *himself on the like Occasion.*

And truly to be just to them who have
written before, the whole serviceableness of
this

To the *English* Gentry.

this small thing doth depend upon and abso-
lutely require a previous frequent Resort to
those Books, which ought never to be out of
the Studies of any School-master, Parent *or*
Tutour *in the Kingdom.*

And though the Management *of my Pro-*
ject can hardly stand the Tryal, yet the
Design *of it will not be censured by any*
man who loves a Gentleman.

I have had Experience how far the
Honour and Interest of Great Families *is*
concerned in the Vertuous Accomplishment of
the Eldest Sons and Heirs : And if the Ob-
servations which mine own Experience hath
forced *me to make are any thing worth, they*
are but a reasonable Acknowledgment of the
Respects which I have received from the
Gentry, both Fathers *and* Sons.

I foresee some Objections which I must
account for.

Object. I. *Why is the Book so short, when*
the Pretensions seem so considerable?

1. *Because I told you that* other Persons
had written before upon one Great Part of
my Subject, to whom I refer you for a thou-
sand wiser Instructions.

2. *I sometimes onely give bare* Hints *of*
serious

To the *English* Gentry.

serious things, when they carry so much Evidence of Reason with them as will make the Active Soul *of any Man who is Good, and desireth to be Wiser, consider and exercise his* Thinking.

3. *I have heard a Wise man say, that there may be as much Judgement required to make a short Book as a long one.*

4. *Suppose the Persons for whose use this is written, should be somewhat Impatient of Reading long things, then perhaps they may be the less displeased with an ordinary Subject, provided they can reade it over at* one sitting.

Object. II. *The* Romantick *manner of Writing.*

Truly, when I was of the Age of those persons in kindness to whom I write, I then thought that Fiction and Intercourse was somewhat more diverting than uniform Narrations *or dogmatical* Propositions. *And I was about to say, that they better understand* Hobbs *his Sense and Principles by* Timothy *and* Philautus, *than from the Grand Authour himself: For there they see Consequences displayed, and the* Slye Connexion *between Dangerous Conclusions and Plausible Pre-*
misses

To the *English* Gentry.

misses exposed, which was palliated before under Good Style and Language, and the Magisterial *Authority of the Proponent.*

Object. III. *The Style sometimes will seem* eager.

Verily this I my self am affraid of, for fear of Indecency (*no man being a competent Judge of his own Indecencies.*)

But two things I have to offer for my self, if the good natur'd Reader will accept of them.

1. *That I do assure him (who am best able) that no* single Person *alive is aimed at or intended to be described and pictured in the angry Characters of a Fond Father, a Womanish Mother, Debauched Son, Wanton Daughter, Ill Schoolmaster, Careless Tutour,* &c. *that would be Rude and Barbarous.*

I set up one of Plato's Idea's, *and sometimes shoot Bitter Words, but this hurts none; there is no Bloud drawn from Universals.*

2. *Whoever thinks the Language Angry; surely, if he would consider well, Sharpness of Style would not be looked upon as more unnecessary for* Instruction, *than pickled Sauces are for* insipid Meat : *'Tis true, they*
grate

To the *English* Gentry.

grate the Palate, but they make the Meat go down, and help Digestion.

Object. IV. *Expressions sometimes* mean, *and Similes too* vulgar : *This I confess my self ashamed of, and is one Reason why I do not put my Name : but really, I knew not how to avoid it ; I knew not how to expose and lessen culpable things, but by* culpable *Language.*

Object. V. *Wandring and hunting out to fetch in* heterogeneous *Matter.*

You may Remember, that I told you before, how impatient *Youth is wont to be, and how to* chain it *I know not, but by various and unexpected Subjects : and there is not any Digression, but some Person or other will be concern'd to understand the Design. And whosoever shall be so kind as to apply the* Instructive *part to his own Use, He is the Man for whom I write, and He onely comprehends my Intention.*

Object. VI. *Why doth it come out at such a time as this ?*

And why not ? No dangerous Design, that I know, is in it, but this, that Gentlemens Sons may hereafter be bred up better than some of their Fathers *have been.*

I have

To the *English* Gentry.

I have oftentimes griev'd, when I have considered the Gallant Youth *of the* English Gentry, *who have as good Parts, and are as well natur'd as any men in* Europe : *and yet as to Learning and Politicks, I am sorry to see some of them turn to so little Account in the Service of King and Countrey.*

This was the Occasion of these Papers ; and when they were first written, a Reverend Divine of Good Estimation hearing them read, was earnest for their Publication : But the frequent Readings over, and continual Reflexions on them glutted my Fancy, *that then it became too familiar, fulsome, and of no Taste : And thence it lay buried in the Dust for several years.*

A while since I fastened upon it with a Fresh Stomach, *and though it did not taste very salt, yet I thought it relished somewhat better than it did before. And having added some few things, I communicated it to a Friend or two on whom I much depend ; they were so complemental as to warrant the good Effect for which it was very sincerely intended ;* Tutouring *being now as necessary (for ought I see) as ever. And those young*

Gentle-

To the *English* Gentry.

Gentlemen are able to read this, who want Age and Solidity *to be affected with Learned Discourses of Controversies and Politicks.*

One thing I heartily beg of the Reader, if any Hint *in these Papers or any* former Discourse *of this kind suggest a Suspicion of the Authour, in the Name of* Friendship, *do not discover him : For at this time, when* Writing, *both as to Substance of Matter and Ornament of Language, is at highest, it is not fit to be subscribed by a man who hath thought away some Years.*

Farwell and be Civil.

THE

T.H E

Guardian's Instruction.

A Letter from a severe Enemy of the University *to his Guardian, a person more moderate, and Member of the Parliament at* Oxford.

SIR,

WE have here the news of another Parliament very speedily at *Oxon*, and, which is more surprising, the Report of your Resolution never to serve as Member more : the Nobility and Gentry will expect some *Account* why a Person who hath served the Government and Religion with that faithfulness and dexterity for above twenty years, should at last be wanting thereunto, when perhaps one *brisk attempt* more might be as much worth as Property and Religion. How you will escape the name of *Tory* I know not, and then it is an easie step to *Papist*. Pray, Sir, rectifie me if I am mistaken by thinking the K. necessitated to call

B   a Para Parliament, by some unexpected emergency either Forein or Domestick : for I do not think the Countrey prepar'd yet :   But if it must be summon'd, why at *Oxford* again ? that *Idle, Ignorant, Ill-bred, Debauch'd, Popish* University of *Oxford* ?   If you do not stand, I am desired to appear, and beg the favour of your Direction towards the management of the *Canvas*, and if I am chosen, towards the management of my self in the *House :*   I had waited upon you my self but that I am confin'd by a great uneasiness contracted by a Cold, and if you fansie my style is grown somewhat more *eager* thereby, do not look upon me as a man uncapable of being better *advised*, but frankly use the Authority which a thousand Circumstances give you over,

Honoured SIR,

Your most obedient

and Affectionate

The

The Answer.

Dear SIR,

THE solitary *Retirement* which I have lately undertaken being Irksome at the first, you could not be more artificial in your Relief, than to engage me in the Answer of a Letter, the substance of which requires more than an ordinary Reflexion, and whereon the Discharge of my thoughts may be *Instructive* as well as *Diverting :* what *Censure* I shall undergo for Declining the Character I have hitherto born, doth not now so much trouble me as it might have done heretofore at your Age, when full of Youth and Heat, coming newly to an Estate and Business, I thought it the speediest Course to be *Considerable,* to appear Haughty and Designing. But now I am grown so much more old than I was forty years agon, that I perfectly contemn censure, which operates no farther than you make it, and which nothing but an unmasculine Timorousness or *slavish* Ambition of Popularity makes considerable. If you measure your self from *abroad,* you must be the cheapest thing alive : I will teach you the true way to *Popularity ;* Let a sincere Design of Honour and Justice be at the Bottom of all your Actions : let an exemplary Piety and Devotion make the world gaze upon you : let no

base

base Words, Actions or Acquaintance lessen the mention of you whereever you come : then may you defie *Censure :* the Good will honor, and the Bad will fear you, you will be applauded by the Wise, and then Fools need not be courted. Whereas on the other side, if you shall forbear an Action fit and *reasonable* merely upon the account of the *Censure* you are likely to undergo (either from the vulgar or great Ones) you will often find it very hard to be *Honest* and *Just.*

There are many *Hindrances* of Justice and Honesty ; *Prejudice, Pride, Malice, Selfishness, Interest* and *Passions,* but none so great as *Cowardice* and *Fear.*

This Humour makes *Princes* flattered, and *Great Ones* never hear their faults : makes Actions of Truth and Justice so *lamely* performed : and is in earnest the very *bane* of all Worth, Honour and Integrity.

But yet I must be so civil to your *Request* as to say, that I am so far from any Contempt of that Honourable way of serving my King and Countrey in Parliament, that I desire never to be valued more for anything in my Life, than for having been in a good measure Instrumental towards the passing some special Bills since the King came in. But I ever thought it unhappy and dangerous for a man to Dye full of *noise* and *business.* And men of *Action* cannot so soon prepare for another Life as *sedentary* men of thought and

and study may. I have ever pitied those men whose necessitous Emploiment and Fortune hath put them under an Obligation of making even at *one* time the *Accounts* of this World and the next. I therefore now fully resolve to narrow my thoughts, and take the advantage which old Age and Experience gives of thinking *strictly*, and reviewing my Life ; and being free'd from fancy (which often cheats the *younger* Judgments) to consider how far the *Rules* I have gon by, how specious soever to others and pleasant to my self, may be consistent with a severe expectation of an *Account* above, where Pleasure, Interest and Passion must disappear. I have procured me many Practical Books of Divinity to assist my untutoured Conceptions, Books of men of all Persuasions : but all do not please me alike : some of them speak *fine* things, but their Meditations are Poetical, Verbose and Fancifull : others are Grave indeed, but they are Learned and *Difficult* when they would instruct : A third sort are Sober, Pious and Easie, but flat, void of all Metal and Spirit, all Cant and *Formality :* A fourth insinuates an *Opinion* he is of.

But another sort of Writers there are with which *this Age* abounds, and which I mainly dwell upon : wherein with simplicity of style and seriousness of thought, I find a *sincere* state of truth and *just* limits of duty, neither too

too loose and large, lest a man should grow
wanton, nor too strict and scrupulous, lest he
should *despair.* And all with a due *movement*
of Passions : out of which I intend to shape
a true *Measure* of my self; learn the *Contempt*
of what hitherto I have admired ; *humble* my
Soul for my many failings, and *warm* my
Devotions by the expectation of a wiser and
better state.

And forasmuch as an universal *Charity* and
compassionate Beneficence to all mankind is
an indispensible Condition of Divine Cle-
mency and the most agreeable Companion
of Mortification : it were barbarous for me
(who Bred you) to let so good a Disposition
goe *unguarded,* which by reason of Youth is
as capable of Direction as it is of Temptation by Prosperity. Therefore take my Experience along with you in the Practice of a
few Rules, by which your great Condition in
the World may become more $\left\{ \begin{array}{l} Easie. \\ Usefull. \end{array} \right\}$

I. More Easie, Quiet, and less Disturb'd.

1. Because true and real Happiness is
within, endeavour for a *solid* Persuasion of *God's Goodness* and Willingness
to pardon sin upon Faith and Repentance and the train of Duties they
imply : for the frequent recurring of
Guilt and unavoidable Infirmities will
beget

beget great solicitousness of thought and dejection of spirit, and if the Devil should suggest *hard* and false notions of God, it may not onely disturb your Happiness, but your Senses too : I would have it a solid *Persuasion,* not the fancifull *Presumption* of every hasty Believer; and upon Terms of the Gospel, to distinguish it from an holy Stupidity, which is as far from true Peace of Conscience as the Sleep procured by *Opiates* is from the *natural* Refreshment of a sound Constitution.

2. Because Fear hath torment, and no torment greater than the Fear of *Death:* make the thoughts of mortality *familiar,* and habituate yourself into a *Capacity* of Dying, this will prevent the great amazement a fit of Sickness many times begets.

3. A Resolution sometimes upon occasion to *deny* your self some satisfactions which your Appetite pursues, though they seem very *reasonable;* then Disappointments and cross Accidents will be easie.

4. Not too much to value the *Censure* of others in the performance of what you apprehend to be your own Duty; neither let Ceremony or Civility at any time hinder *Business.*

5. Not to be discouraged in your Duty by
the

the foresight or opinion of *Unsuccess-fulness.*

6. If you are complying and of an easie Temper ; not to be hasty and lavish of Promises, the Performance may be troublesome.

7. If of a gratefull Temper, not to accept of unnecessary Favours, the thoughts of Requital are afflicting.

8. If of a good natur'd pitying Disposition, not to be *unwarily free* to Strangers or Relations of *mean* fortune, lest they *crave* too much, and think all you have their due.

9. If *melancholy ;* to labour against it, as the Parent of $\left\{ \begin{array}{l} \text{Fears} \\ \text{Scruples} \end{array} \right\}$ which are *vexatious* and endless.

10. If *proud ;* to consider, it will create Envy, Contempt and Design, and is really the greatest Folly, and yet we are all marvellously subject to it.

11. If *passionate ;* to study the Prevention of the obvious *Occasions,* consider the *Indecency* and the many *Disturbances* of it, to be always on your *guard* for fear.

12. If *given to women,* consider the Shame and Scandal, and slavish fear of Dis-covery.

13. If *malitious ;* to consider the Enmity and Danger it begets, and that you must

must forgive, if you hope to be for-
given.

14. If *disputatious;* to consider how dis-
obliging and uncivil it seems.

15. Not to be *inquisitive* into Secrets or
meddling in other mens Affairs you
are not concerned with. Not to be
always asking *Questions* in Company,
it is ill *Breeding.*

16. Not to contend with *Great* ones, but
quickly yield, whatever be the Provo-
cation : They will *worst* you at last.

17. Not to name or reflect on Persons in
promiscuous Company : You know not
their *Relations,* or whom you disoblige.

18. Not to believe every man you converse
with as *honest* as your self, upon a
friendly and complaisant Address :
The World is a great *Cheat.*

19. Not to be *ashamed* to ask pardon of
whom you have injured, and make
what *restitution* you are capable of.

20. Not to be too *open* and free of conversation (whatever be your Wit) and
how pleasant soever you may seem to
Company, they will contemn you, and
may *mischief* you afterwards.

21. Not to be too *wary* and cautious in your
Opinion of small things, amongst wise
men : this looks like suspicion and is
ridiculous to *whisper* Proclamations,
and

and not tell a man what day of the month it is, without *considering*, this is formal and foppish.

22. Not *hastily* to think any man your Enemy, it may *make* one, a man may be *angry* with you, and not *hate* you.

23. Not to *trust* one whom you have disoblig'd, too soon.

24. To expect and resolve to *bear* with many Offences and Indignities, and consider that no condition of Life can be free from all *disquiet,* for ought I know, it would be *dangerous.*

25. Not *easily* to believe Reports concerning your self or others.

26. Not quickly to espouse the *Quarrels* of your Relations or Friends.

27. Beware of being too much obliged by *Great men,* they will be apt to impose Hardships upon you, it may prove a *slavery* to you, if they are *proud.*

28. Beware of setting up that *stirdy Resolution* which some make, never to give off what they have once begun, but at all adventures to go on; this may run you into vast inconveniencies.

29. Be cautious of undertaking greater Designs than what are just and sutable to your *Condition ;* then if you miscarry, you will not be *contemned.*

30. Be carefull to treasure up the *Remembrance* of all God's mercies to you and yours :

yours : For Gratitude is a good *Guard* against sin, *Gen.* 39. 9.

31. In time of great Crosses and Affliction, be sure *first* to pray for *Pardon* of sin, and then you may with Earnestness and hopes beg *Pity*, Matt. 9. 2, 5, 6. Is. 59. 1, 2.

32. When you pray for Pardon of sins, because we all *forget* many sins we would repent of, if we thought on them, be carefull to mention *secret* and *forgotten* sins.

33. You must resolve to *marry ;* for to leave the management of your great Family to *Servants* onely, is neither for Credit or Profit, and to undertake all the little things of House-keeping your self, will be Gossiping : Beside the dull converse of *Servants* onely, will either give Scandal, or tempt you to *ramble*, and make you be thought looser than really you are.

34. If circumstances will permit, put yourself into the state of Life, which most agrees with your *Temper.*

35. Do not accustom your self (be your *riches* what they will) to be too *nice*, curious and fantastical in *Diet, Habit, Attendance*, that will prove very troublesome.

36. Be not extravagantly high in expression of your *Commendations* of men you like.

37. Study

37. Study and pray for a perfect *Resignation* of your will to God's will, and with all imaginable *Application* of mind say, Not my will, but thy Will be done ; and then go, be as happy as you please.

II. Your Life is also to be *Usefull* to others as well as *Easie* to your self.

1. By the good *Example* of a vertuous and holy Life ; Incredible is the Influence of a *great Man* on a Family, Parish and Neighbourhood : for the Vulgar have quite lost their *Hearing ;* Preaching is but an honester sort of *Diversion :* they learn all by gaping and staring on a man in fine Clothes. And therefore since you can so *easily* doe God and Man so great service, pray look on your self *obliged.* Do not put God off with a little *fashionable* Civility to the national Religion. I am afraid the serious *Reflecting* and *Meditating* part is not frequent enough among the Gentry. Let not Pastime, Business or Company *waste* all the day : Retire a little and *Enjoy* your own Soul. This will not lessen the Pleasures of Life but sweeten and make them *solid ;* and make them differ from the crack-

crackling of *Thorns* and the flame of *Straw.* I mean the thin, short-liv'd delights of the *boysterous* part of the world.

2. *Knowledge.* Great are the Advantages which the Wealth of the Gentry affords them for Knowledge : they are capable thereby of the choicest *Education,* greatest variety of usefull *Books* and learned'st *Companions* in study. But one sort of knowledge above all the rest will render them exceeding serviceable in the places where they live, (a considerable knowledge in the *Law*) beside the pleasure that study would afford, as copying out the *Reason* and *Wisdom* of the Nation. This will make them more securely possess and prudentially manage their Estates for their Posterity. And what service may they doe others by untying knots and composing differences ? By hindring men from suffering Oppression by *Ignorance ;* by directing the management of Parochial and Countrey *Business ;* which the general road men go in doth not safely shew.

3. *Power.* What should hinder the Master of a Family from keeping his Servants duly to Prayers at home, and in their turns to Sermons and Sacraments at Church ? What an *Empire* hath a
Justice

Justice of Peace in the Countrey! and how *gallantly* is that Power bestowed when an extravagant Ale house is *unlicensed*, a common Swearer *fined*, an useless Vagabond forced to *work*, a quarrelsome Neighbour reduced to *manners*, and a poor abused Minister is *assisted* ? at what a mighty *rate* doth the Judge sell every minute wherein *righteous* Judgment is given ; the Cause of the *Widow* patiently heard, and the fraud and wit of the *Oppressour* over-ruled ? When the Bribery, Perjury and Malice of a *Witness* is condemn'd, and the *greatest Man* that offends afraid to come before him.

4. By *Wealth.* It is an ill-natur'd sort of Doctrine to preach, and will not hold at *Westminster*, that the *Poor* have a good *Title* to some of the rich man's Money : But it would be an unlucky *Disappointment* hereafter, if in stead of asking how many Lordships you left your Heir, How many Daughters you married to great Fortunes, How many Livery-men you kept, *&c.* God should demand, How many poor Widows have you sav'd from *starving* ? How many Labourers you have set to work and paid *honestly :* how many *decay'd* Families you have reliev'd ; what did you give to a *Brief* for a Fire, Church, or

or Hospital, *&c.* Reade *Barrow* of Charity. The practice of these Rules will help qualifie a Life of Action such as yours much be, and mine hath been.

But now I bid adieu to all *publick Affairs :* this Nation will never want a breed of men to manage its *Concerns.*

As for the next thing, *The King's being under the necessity of a Parliament.*

I know no necessity can be upon the King to call a Parliament but a Forein *War* and want of *Money :* As for a War, 'tis not likely (unless by the *Moors* upon *Tangier*) we have attempted to play the King at *France,* but they two will hardly meddle with one another ; we have endeavoured to make *Spain* break with us, but they are *poor,* the *Dutch* are *cunning,* so that his Majesty is secure in that point. As for want of Money, it is said and believed that the King is now made a good Husband, and hath money in the Che-quer : if so, it will bring down the price of Membership : We had been better to have given him a million of money than to have suffered him ever to come to *Think* and grow cunning ; for, if I ken him aright, he hath Parts enough to govern a bigger Nation than this, if he can once endure the penance of *Business* and leave off to be afraid of meeting

us

us at *Westminster.* And it is probable he never will be so again, since the Success of that Venture of Contempt upon us, in the amazing *precipitated* dissolution at *Oxford;* from which time I will be bold to date the sinking of *Parliamentary* Grandieur.

I guess who it was within one man or two who for interest and security thought it necessary that things should be put to some *issue* at *Oxford,* the City being embittered by the removal of us, and things carried so high as to force the King either to shew Fear and yield to *terms;* or Fury, and so act a severe part upon some Members, and by that give occasion to a Tumult in the City, which then certainly was design'd.

Whereas you question the King's *Interest in the Countrey,* let me tell you, I perceive the Countrey cools apace, and he who deals with the Vulgar must doe his business quickly, for seven hours sleep will make a Clown *forget* his design. It hath been no small advantage to the King that his Adversaries still act with more *noise* and *tumult* than he : and though noise and tumult does wonders while it continues, yet when it once sinks and grows calm, it is far more difficult to be usefull again. I take the Vulgar to be like a *Race-horse,* when he is upon speed it is a mighty pace, but if in the course he be checked and comes to *trot* it is very hard to make him gallop again.

If

If a Parliament must be summon'd, yet
why at *Oxford?*   *Idle, Ill-bread, Ignorant, Debauch'd Popish Oxford?*

You will wonder how I should come to be
an Advocate for *Oxford*, who have railed at it
for above forty years together, and perhaps
upon better grounds than most men do.

I was entred there when the first great
difficulties arose betwixt the old King and
Parliament, and as much care was taken as
was usual in the choice of a Tutour : But as
I came to understand there was a certain
Master of Arts who was to be the next
Tutour of course, and so the next Gentleman
who entred was to be recommended to him
in his turn, it happened I was the man, who
came with tolerable Parts and Learning at
the rate of a Gentleman ; I had a great
reverence for the Person who was to be my
Guide, and a strong opinion to be made very
wise.

It happened that my Tutour was a great
Philosopher, which made me proud to hear
of, expecting in some short time to be so
too : He began at first *gloriously* with me, to
magnifie the advantages of a good Education : How the greatest Conditions of *Honour*
and *Trust* were supplied from the University :
What a disgrace it was to the Nation, and
what an injury to Government of Church

C   and

and State, that when other Countries, *France,
Poland, Scotland,* &c. are studious to discipline
their Nobility and Gentry into *good Manners,
Politicks* and *Religion,* here eldest Sons are
generally condemned to Hawks and Hounds,
and Wisedom left the Patrimony of *younger*
Brothers onely, and *Poor* mens Sons : That
the mutual lustre of a Diamond beset with
Gold was a mean *Comparison* to Wisedom in
the breast of such a man as I. This ravished
my rustick modesty, and made me proud
with the thoughts of what I should hereafter
be.   I out-waked the Bell, and scorned to
be called to my Duty.   I attended every
motion of his Eye for a summons to Philosophy, and thought every minute an hour
till I was entred into that course of study,
which was to make me and all my Relations happy.   But alas! the fame of his
Parts and Learning had gained him Acquaintance whose company was dearer than mine;
so that a Lecture now and then was a great
Condescention, and I most days in the week,
when others were carefully looked after, left
naked to infinite temptations of doing nothing, or worse ; but God's *Grace,* the good
Example of my Parents and a *natural* Love of
Vertue, secured me so far as to leave *Oxford*
(the troubles coming on) though not much
more learned, yet not much worse than I
came thither : I must in justice say in favour
of the University in general, that the growing
disturb-

disturbances in Church and State, and some Disputes in the University, may well be supposed an unhappy occasion of slackening the *Discipline* there at that time.

But this infinite *Disappointment* did so afflict me, that when I came to have Children, I did almost *swear* them in their Childhood never to be friends with *Oxford.* This peevishness of mine was much increased by a Chaplain of my Sister's, who was made a Fellow of a College in the late times, and turned out upon the Restauration of the King. He sought occasions continually to rail at the University for Ignorance, Debauchery and Irreligion, insomuch that I sent my eldest Son abroad, to try what improvement might be gained by travelling ; at least to divert. I would willingly have sent him to the *Inns of Court* but that I had observed for these last twenty years how the Gaiety and Frolick of the Court, and the great admiration of Wit, had softned the Souls of many excellent Persons into an aversion from Industry ; who made themselves no otherwise considerable than for assisting at a Ball, and instead of adding Wealth and Honour to a Family by advancement through the Law, impaired both ; and, which is most deplorable of all, at length came off poisoned with such a licentiousness of Manners, shameless Atheism, and heathenish promiscuous use of Women, that either Gentlemen

C 2   could

could not persuade their eldest Sons to (the *Confinement* of) Marriage, or scarce find Ladies of Fortune and Quality which dared to venture to have them for *Husbands.*

Nothing but such Reasons as these can justifie my venturing my eldest Son so *early* into the wide world : And I must confess, that when he returned from beyond Sea, I was pleased to see the ruff boyish humour *filed* a little, and shaped into much of a Man. I was infinitely delighted with the prospect of the Happiness I promised my self in the Conversation of an Heir who brought home the same *Innocence* of Inclinations he carried, and by *staring* about *France* and *Italy,* had furnished himself with a *Complaisance* very acceptable whereever he came.

But you must pardon two qualities he had contracted.   1. An humour of magnifying things abroad in comparison with his own Countrey.   2. A *stateliness* of behaviour, and contempt of mean Acquaintance.   The last of these I did not much discourage, finding him Just and Charitable.   For I have often seen young Gentlemen guarded from low and base Actions and Company by *generosity* of Spirit.   And how many men do you and I know, loose enough (God help them) from the *Bigotry* of Conscience, and yet upon the bare *Religion* of Honour rather than disgrace a worthy *Family*, misbecome a *Character*, or fail the *opinion* of the World, do as much
scorn

scorn a base Action, will be as true to their Word, when they might gain by Lying ; as far from cheating a Widow, Minister, or Orphan, who cannot contend, or doe any ungenteele thing, as that man who thinks the world to come worth *twenty* of these.

But (Nephew) you are *Rich* and *Great*, and therefore I must have a care you do not mistake me, when I say I would have my eldest Son a little *stately;* I do not mean any degree of that *gross* imperious Pride which God and Man *hates :* That first-born Monster of *Selfishness,* and ill-natur'd Complexion of the *Devil :* Poison'd and puff'd up with *Envy* of what Equals and Betters enjoy ; which makes a man think all the World made for his *single* Lust and Pleasure : *Overlook* Mankind, *Rebell* against Superiours, *Malitious* to Equals, *Tyrant* to Inferiours, *Merciless* to the Offendour, *Cruel* to the Needy and *False* to the Hireling: Kind onely to *Sycophants,* and Friend to *None :* Walk, Spread and Swell like the mighty builder of *Babylon* when he was turning *Brute.*

And not onely the *Vileness* of the Sin makes the Proud Man as sure to be Hated in this World as he is to be Damn'd in the next ; but the Proud Man is a greater *Fool* than I believe he thinks *himself :* For he loseth what he mainly aims at, instead of being Honour'd and Esteem'd, he makes himself the most *Contemptible* thing alive. For he is discovered

by

by all his Words, Actions and Designs, even when he *counterfeits* Humility and Obliging-ness ; oh how 'tis *overdone*, strain'd and formal.   It was always thought a great mea-sure of Folly to be *able* to be Flattered : and of all men living if you meet with a Proud Man, you have him at your *mercy :* It is but to magnifie his *Ancient* Family, though per-haps his Great Grandfather could not Write and Reade ; The Splendour of his *Living*, when perhaps the hired Liverymen dare not drink once in a month in his House : His *Wit*, when perhaps it is most shewn by hold-ing his tongue, *&c.* doe but all this and keep your *Countenance*, ask what you will he never denies the man who understands Worth. And you must be sure also to tune your *cringing* Muscles by a French Fiddle, *Shrugg*, and make your honour punctually, you may lead the great Thing to and fro as if he had a *Ring* in his Nose.

But to come to my *Son* again.   It quickly appear'd how *sad* is the *condition* of a Gentle-man without *Learning*.   For wanting some ingenuous Diversion to fill the *deal* of void time young Gentlemen have in the Countrey, and being ashamed to be still obliged to *Silence* in all discourses of Learning and State, for want of more Knowledge ; he fell into such an *immoderate* love of Sports that he was never well but when he was managing or talking of his Dogs ; and in a little time

became

became fit company for *nothing* else : Debauched, and wholly *useless* to King, Countrey and his Family, and if I had not been alive to secure the Estate, he prov'd as likely to have made a Gentleman of his Steward as any Man in *England.*

I know I am blam'd (but my Wife must bear her share) for breeding him up at a *mean School :* For she pretending the danger in *great Schools* of growing a man too soon, and learning ill Tricks (but *in Truth* because this place was *near,* and she could see him and hear from him *often*) would hear of no other Master.

And really the Countrey Gentlemen are somewhat hardly dealt withall *in this point :* For sometimes very mean Persons are licensed to ruine our Children, to the great Prejudice of Church and State, a Schoolmaster being the best or worst Subject in the Nation : not but that we have now as many worthy Schoolmasters as ever, but one ignorant one doth mischief enough.

The Parliament hath used all the prudent Caution imaginable, by referring that Affair to the Inspection of the *Ordinary :* It cannot be objected that we do not give *encouragement* enough to maintain fit persons; for I am bold to say, no Gentleman is so *weak* as not *Plentifully* to gratifie that Person, who is to contribute to the Prosperity of a whole *Family,* by spending all his Thoughts, Pains and Time
in

in studying the *various* Tempers and Inclinations of Youth as he must doe, if he will be *just* to our Expectations.

But very mean was that Person to whom I sent my Son upon my Wife's *Importunity.*

And perhaps hereafter you may find it a very hard matter, not to be guided by a *Wife* in the *breeding* your Children. For that Fondness which is a *just debt* from all to a Wife, and is in some by Nature excessive, if she be cunning enough to humour it well with a few Tears or a pretended Fit, will melt your sweet Disposition. Mistake me not, I speak this onely by way of *Caution*, that when you marry and grow fond, you may manage your *uxoriousness* more warily than I have done, for your own Credit and the good of your Children.

I do not speak this to *discourage Marriage.* For I will sincerely aver, that where the choice of *Quality*, *Temper* and *Fortune* is tolerably prudent, there is a great deal more Happiness than in a discontented, loose, unsatisfied *single Life*, unless to those Persons whose Callings oblige them to a continual *Thoughtfulness* and moderation of *Diet.*

I cannot but speak upon this Subject with a great *Concern.* For, I believe, if I had married my Son immediately after his return from *Travel*, while he was a *stranger* to bad Company and the Vices in *fashion*, I might have prevented his Extravagances, and fixed
the

the *Mercury*. But afterwards, too late, when I had provided an agreeable Match, his Comrades had instilled into him such an *Aversion*, and taught him to rail at Matrimony in the Language of the *Stews*, that the *design* of Happiness to my Family was utterly defeated : And once, I remember, full of Grief upon that Account, I was visited by a Friend who condoled the mischief of such *evil Principles*, and the sinfull Consequences of them. And, the better to relieve the burthen I was oppressed with, and prate some of ·my *Thoughtfulness* away; I ask'd him, what he conceived were the Occasions of the present great *Contempt* of *Matrimony*. He smiled, and told me, that he had no great skill in the Business of Matrimony, but the Contempt of it, he thought, arose,

1. From the Influence the Devil hath upon the wild Libertinism of Nature, for want of the Fear of God, *Gen.* 20. 11. and our cross-grain'd Appetite still to the *Forbidden-fruit*.

2. The frequency of leud Examples, which have baffled the *Courage* ·of Ecclesiastical Censure.

3. The popular notion of Matrimony being a slavish *confinement :* It is voluntary and therefore the less to be complain'd of, and sometimes it proves better to have business to doe than to be *idle ;* An Huntsman, no doubt,
if

if he should see a Shopkeeper walk-
ing all the day long in a little Room,
would think it a *damnable confinement*,
and the other man makes it his *happiness.*

4. The Women govern: The wiser they:
But I fansie that the Women never
govern where the Man hath *Wit*
enough to doe it himself; and I hope
you would not have Government *dye?*

5. False notions of the Instances and
Allowances in the Old Testament.

6. Some peevish Expressions against Marriage in the good old primitive *Fathers*,
not to say any thing of *modern Writers*.

7. The barbarous *forcing* Matches upon
Children without their own Consent,
and sad Consequences of that.

8. The everlasting Din of *Mothers-in-law.*

9. The hard-usage of the first brood, if
they marry again.

10. The Railery of such who either volun-
tarily *undertake* Cœlibacy, or whose
Condition of Life obligeth them to it.

11. The easie Cure of the French Complement, otherwise the sense of Honour
and care of Health would make many
a Gentleman like his *Own* Lodging.

There are many other Reasons of the
Contempt of Matrimony which you may
find in the *Lady's Calling*, and in another
(waggish) book which I dare not name for
fear

fear of displeasing an excellent Mistress I have in the World, and because, I hope, he wrongs *new married* Ladies. These (Nephew) we both agreed, were the common Occasions of that Contempt under which Matrimony now labours, to the great Inconvenience of the Nation by *Immorality*, to Families for want of *Heirs*, and good young Ladies for want of *Husbands.*

This I thought fit to write to you; for whom we have provided an admirable Match, a Lady of all the good Qualities I would desire if I were of your Age. She is very Beautifull, and not *Proud ;* She is Well-shap'd, and not *Stiff ;* She is Witty, and not *Impertinent ;* She is Familiar, but not *Fond ;* Good-natur'd, but not *Easie ;* Rich, but not *Imperious;* Young, but not *Foolish ;* Religious, but not *Fantastical :* She wants but one good Character more, that is, being *Your Wife.* And, I hope, we shall not find you so diffi-cult to the wishes of your best Friends as my ungovernable Son, my incurable Son hath prov'd, utterly undone for want of *Education.*

But (God be thanked) a better Instruc-tion fell to your Share : And though I was against your going to *Oxford,* yet the little time you spent there was to so good pur-pose, that I am sorry for the Occasion of your not continuing longer, (which I per-ceive you will never forgive the University.)
But

But now it may be hoped that you are of Age to consider, that *Conscience* and *Care* could not but oblige the Head of your House and Tutour to send home the first Alarm of Danger, when a Person of so great Hopes and Fortune, out of Youth and Goodness of Disposition, was like to become a Prey: Sure I am, the sense of Vertue and Religion and industrious Inclinations you brought thence deserves thanks, which my Son wanted, thanks to a foolish Father and Mother.

Well whether I or my Wife were most guilty it is now onely matter of *Repentance;* But our School-master (as appeared) by reason of Ignorance was never able to proceed to a *Degree* in the University, and set up his Staff for a Livelihood which fell toward a Countrey School. He riggs himself out with a new Suit, broad Hat and Silver headed Staff, and being Secure from all Censure in point of Learning, his business with us was onely to counterfeit a *wise* and a *good man,* the first he gained the esteem of by an affected Gravity and a wary Silence in Company; the second he was secure of in our Countrey, by acting an extraordinary *Preciseness* and disgusting the imposed use of Ceremonies, confounding the Order of Bishop and Presbyter, magnifying the Advantages of a Commonwealth, railing at the Bishops Courts, and pitying the Hardships
of

of taking Oaths, and being forced to Church. And having Wit enough to *cringe* to every Person, and comply with his Betters in all Discourse without the least *Contradiction*, he gain'd the Character of an *humble* and meek man. So that now Emploiment quickly came on, and happy was the Gentleman who could welcome this great *Gamaliel* with the first tender of his Respect, that is, the Sacrifice of an *eldest Son.*

Being settled in his Dominion, lest the forementioned humility and want of Learning (which Children are apt to smell out) should end in Contempt. He puts on a great self-conceit, ruffles amongst the trembling Boys with a *Fantastical Imperiousness,* and procures the name of a strict and carefull man by a partial Cruelty to poor mens children, for he knew Mothers had somewhat as sovereign as Crabbs-eyes to sweeten the Choler, lest the dearly beloved eldest Son should come to a mischance.

For a long time I stood by and look'd on, but my Wife did so *hale* and *pull* me to send my Child to so *near* a School, that I saw no hopes of Peace, till I complied ; I had the Flattery of several years of the Dutifulness and Proficiency of my Son, which my Wife never doubted of, seeing her Son kept sweet, neat. in Cloaths and *sheepish,* (which she called good-manners.) This Sheepishness, or over Bashfulness of his, I was troubled at,

at, and endeavoured to mend, because of an
Accident which I knew had befallen a young
Gentleman my Neighbour: He was a genteel Youth, very fine in Parts and Disposition; his *Mother* was sensible of this, and
fond enough; and so jealous of every Action,
imperious and rigid to an hair's breadth of
Duty, loud and noisy at every small mis-
carriage, (and sometimes at none.) This
made the neat Youth dread the place whereever his Mother was: *timorously* perform
every Duty for fear of being chidden, and at
last so far dispirited, that when he grew up,
and for Age and Knowledge was thought fit
to be courted by the best sort of Acquaintance, he was quite over-grown with that
Curb of *just* and *publick* Actions call'd *Infirmi-
tas frontis;* he would behave himself so diffi-
dently, that sense and words would fail him;
and if his Mother came into the Room he
was presently struck dumb.

Another Youth (exactly such) I knew
whose Schoolmaster was rough and hasty,
so that whenever he came into the School
the gentle Boy trembled, his heart constantly
aked for fear, and at last contracted such an
incurable Hectick as destroyed him.

These two Instances give me an unavoidable occasion of recommending the Practice
of the Schoolmaster I was bred up under:
He was a plain man, skill'd in his Profession,
industrious and undesigning. His way was
this;

this; First to sift the Temper of every Youth;
If he found a Boy *ruggish and untractable*,
quickly to ease himself of the uncomfort-
able duty of Severity : But if they were
tractable and easie, whatever were their
Parts or Learning, to make the best of both,
encourage the Children with *Civility* and
Kindness : He knew there was a *Generosity* in
Gentlemen, and that what Imperiousness
could not doe, Courtesie might, and out of
Gratitude and a sense of Love and Care, he
found better success than if he had affrighted
them into Duty.

Well, when my Boy grew toward a Man,
I took him away, and upon Examination I
found that he had sent me home nothing but
the very shell of a Gentleman, spruce indeed
in habit, handsome and well-natur'd, but infinitely void of all Knowledge either of words
or things. It is true, I got him turn'd out,
but in the mean time, my hopes were lost,
so that it became no small Concern of mine
to take better Care for the *second Son*, who
had smarted for a better share of Learning
somewhat than his Brother, at a *greater
School*. Him therefore I was resolved not
to *condemn* (as Gentlemen phrase it) but to
prefer to a *Profession*. But what Course to
take I was at a loss. *Cambridge* was so far
off, I could not have any Eye upon him,
Oxford I was *angry* with.

There was in the Neighbourhood an old
grave

grave Learned Divine (a rigid Churchman) and therefore thought me not zealous enough: but yet the great Integrity and Simplicity of his Life, and the Inoffensiveness of a free converse in matters of Indifferency, was Reason enough to me of standing by his *Judgment* in this great *Confusion* of mine own thoughts.

I desired his advice in the choice of a Profession, for I thought the Gentry and Nobility of this Nation the most *mistaken* men alive.

First, for breeding the elder and younger Sons at one *common* idle rate, as if both were to inherit equally, so that afterwards when they grow Men, and a Distinction must of necessity be made, it always breeds ill Bloud, and sometimes proves dangerous.

Secondly, for thinking it somewhat *beneath* Persons of Quality to gain a Livelihood by the industry of a Profession, such as a Child's inclination points to.

Physick we both did own to be in the speculation very *pleasant*, and in the Practice *gainfull*, but forasmuch as Eminency in that Study requires a more than ordinary Knowledge in many sorts of Learning, and is so full of Care and Hardship, we left that to such who were furnished with more Learning, and invited by a strong natural Propensity thereunto.

Civil Law was then proposed as a genteel
sort

sort of Study, but when I considered into how few hands the Gains of that Profession falls, and how few Offices of Preferment there are, I laid aside all thoughts of that Learning, though most *honourable* of any next to Divinity.

My Neighbour spake well and largely of Divinity ; and such was the *honesty* and clearness of his humour, that he frankly told me, that I, not favouring Episcopacy much, would hardly encourage a Son to be a Divine : I was not angry with his *undesigning* plainness, but grievously afflicted not to be more truly known to him ; and with some kind of trouble in spirit I made him my Confessour. I told him,

That it did please God out of a sense of humane infirmity, I was naturally of a disposition prone to great *Pity* and *Compassion* to such as were poor, most of all to such as I saw honest in their morals, and, as I thought, sincere in Religion. And that once (out of *Curiosity*) I went to a notorious Meeting, upon the fame of an extraordinary gifted Preacher. I would, I confess, willingly, being a Member of that Parliament (which made the Act of Uniformity) have *contracted* my self, and not have been known to appear so much in opposition to it, but that could not be ; and yet I was resolved to see what matter of *moment* there was to encourage my favouring of Dissenters, being born of Parents
D

who

who paid dear for their Loyalty in the late times.

When the Meeters had given me the *invidious* unacceptable Deference of place, up springs a man with a briskness of look, fit to have domineer'd in the best Auditory in *England.* He throws his gaping Eyes about upon the numerous throng. He had no sooner named his Text, but about the Leaves and the Blew Strings of the *Dutch Bibles* flew, happy was the man who spit upon his Thumb, and first found the Chapter.

He began (I suppose upon a *mistake* of his Auditory) with Address, Language, Rhetorick, and thought as if he had been an Angel; and I never in all my life time prepared my self so much for attention; no not in the House of Commons: But he, *correcting* himself, descended to such a lamentable meanness of Looks, Words and Thoughts, a plainly affected Wink, Shrugg and Whine, that I was altogether as much ashamed to be a Witness of what the Women sigh'd at and admir'd: and coming home to my Lodging, sent to speak one word with the Preacher, who enquiring what I was; and understanding me a *member* of Parliament, shifted his Lodgings.

This afterwards I complained of in the House of Commons, freely confessing my Curiosity, and excusing the same by the
Design

Design I had in it. But I perceived that some of the most clamorous Members against Conventicles laughed at the Story, and found out business of another kind to stop any reflexion upon the Circumstances I related, from which time I began to be *jealous* of Conventicles, which before I *pitied.*

I went on, and told him farther, that, I thought, if at the *Restauration* some things had been left out of the Liturgy and others added, it might perhaps have bated many *exceptions* which are now made, but never in my Life thought an Alteration of it *afterwards* safe for the Kingdom.

That I go to Church with as much *Affection* as any man breathing, admire the *simple, full* and *significant* style of the Liturgy, and the distinction of short Collects as an ease to *tyred* Devotion ; Pictures in Churches and frequent bowings I never was fond of, but as a Gentleman of breeding where-ever I saw others bow I did so too, thinking singularity *stiff* and *ungenteel.*

And as for change of the *Monarchy* into a Common-wealth, I scarce ever heard, I am sure never endured, any Discourse tending that way. Alas ! I remember the Protectorship of a fortunate *Officer,* and the Tyranny of *Major-Generals :* and were not I fit to be begged for a Madman or a Fool, if I should encourage a Tumult wherein 'tis Cross and Pile but some Varlet or other whom I have

laid

laid by the *Heels* for tearing Hedges, shall
swagger at the head of twenty men worse
than he, rob my Study, fire my House,
ravish my Children and cut my Throat?

Let the faults of Governours (said I) and
Government be what they will, it is much
safer to bear these faults than to venture a
Change: which I confess many an innocent
undesigning man may contribute to *accidentally*, but on purpose and studiously, none
but such as either disgorged King and
Church Lands at the Restauration, or such
as fail'd in expectation of great Places, or
were dispossessed from them, or such whose
Vices have consumed a large Patrimony,
and disgraced an ancient Family, shall
attempt a *Reparation* from King or Church:
all which I and my Ancestours have ever
abhorred; and now said I, Sir, with the
great freedom you began, pray tell me what
I am sick of, that the best Churchmen
should bid such a man as I stand off, and
cry *unclean, unclean.*

Upon this the honest man replied, that I
was a better Church of *England* man than
himself: And yet notwithstanding all this,
I was resolved against making my Son a
Divine, though for reasons not to the dis-
credit but to the *honour* of the Church.

I look on it (said I) as an incomparable
advantage of that Profession to have for its
single especial *Calling* what is the concern
of

of all mankind, namely the study of the knowledge of our duty toward God and Man : from which all other *Professions*, some more, some less, afford great Avocations and incredible *Hinderances.* Nay, if *temporal* advantages were a man's design, a Child could not be placed in more probable circumstances (having Friends to lend a helping hand) of an early plentifull fortune than holy Orders. And having mentioned the Temporal Advantages of the Clergy, I cannot forbear on this occasion giving you, Nephew, my advice concerning the disposal of your great Living of *C.* which I am told is likely to be void by the death of the Doctour who is now past all hopes of Recovery. You must expect infinite *solicitations* when so great a preferment falls ; and if you have any value for one who resolves to spend all his wisedom upon you, let me beg you to act like an English Gentleman : it is reported that Master *H.* your Bailiff hath a Kinsman very fit to be recommended : Others say that your Mother's Nurse's Daughter knows a man very deserving ; and some report that his Grace the D. of ―― intends to oblige you by giving you this fair occasion of owning the favour of his Grace's condescension to be acquainted with you, by making his Friend Rectour of 500*li.* a year. Come, come, act like a man who understands and deserves the true

name

name of *Patron*, that is wisely dispose the
Living, and then *Protect* the Minister in his
Rights and Privileges, neither *wrong* him
your self nor suffer others to doe it :   Do
not hamper him and call him ungratefull
fellow if he refuse to compound for *twenty
per Cent.*   Perhaps while you are warm with
Pride and Prosperity Repentance may look
cowardly and Restitution ungenteel.   Acts
of Injustice may *go down easily*, but they will
rattle in your throat when you come to die.
You are secure from my begging, for my
Son shall not be a Divine ; for in truth the
Knowledge real or pretended of Scripture
and Divinity which the wise sort of all Professions now *pretend* to, and the great *Controversies* and variety of opinions which of
late have been set on foot, make it absolutely necessary for a Divine to be furnished
with deeper Learning than ordinary, and the
want of *strictness* in the Education of a Son
of a great Family, will render the *confinement*
in that severe Profession irksome to such a
Youth as mine, and without which he can
never *adorn* his Function.

At last I *plainly* owned that the Common
Law was my design, having observed that
critical Learning was not required, and I
desired my Neighbour's opinion and direction hereunto.   He did confess
That he thought it a study so *laudable*
that he would willingly have spent some
time

time in it himself but that the loss of so much time must needs have intrench'd upon his proper *Calling*.

He look'd upon each great Lawyer capable of signal service to the *State* and infinite Acts of *Charity* to private Persons; and that it must be impossible twenty years hence for a good Lawyer to want *Preferment*. But he offered *many things* to be considered before the Law was to be attempted.

1. Whether my Son had *strength* of Constitution to undergo the drudgery of six or seven years close study?

2. Whether living in an University as a *Gentleman* at large without close confinement would not habituate him to *Laziness* greater than that study is consistent with.

3. Great care must be taken to give him sound Notions of Justice and Charity. Because, though neither the Law nor any other Profession brings any necessity on a man or irresistible temptations to be injurious, yet in all Professions there are some, and in the Law, from the shew of Parts being able to carry a doubtfull Cause: And I verily believe (said he) that many a good man at the hour of death doth repent of having served the interest of an ill Suit, notwithstanding the excuse of being obliged by the *Calling* to speak, having

having received his Fee. After all this, if I did stand it out in favour of the Law, then Logick, for a year or two in some University would be usefull, because frequent formal disputation makes a Youth more *attentive* to a Discourse and more quickly apprehensive of a false or weak Reasoning.

And when I objected my Prejudice against *Oxford,* from my own experience formerly, and from the suggestions of my Sister's Chaplain just before and after the King came in: the first he could not answer for, the latter he confessed in part was true at the time it points out.

For of all places the University being *fast* to the Monarchy, suffering most and being most weary of the Usurpation, when *Oliver* was dead, and *Richard* dismounted, they saw through a maze of Changes, that in little time the Nation would be fond of that Government which twenty years before they hated. The hopes of this made the Scholars talk aloud, drink healths, and curse *Meroz* in the very Streets : Insomuch that when the King came in, nay, when the King was but *voted* in, they were not onely like them that dream, but like them who are out of their wits, mad, stark staring mad ; to study was *Fanaticism,* to be moderate was down-right *Rebellion,* and thus it continued for a twelvemonth, and thus it would have continued till
this

this time, if it had not pleased God to raise up some Vice-Chancellours who stemmed the torrent which carried so much filth with it, and in defiance of the loyal zeal of the *Learned*, the drunken zeal of *Dunces*, and the great amazement of *young Gentlemen*, who really knew not what they would have, but yet made the greatest noise, reduced the University to that temperament that a man might study and not be thought a *Dullard*, might be sober and yet a *Conformist*, a Scholar and yet a *Church of England-man ;* and from that time the University became sober, modest and studious as perhaps any *University* in *Europe.*

And if after all this I thought well of an University, he advised me not to *avoid* this or that House, because a vicious debauch'd Person came thence, not to be *fond* of an House because I my self was of it, or because the Head thereof was a fam'd man : these (said he) many times prove very fallacious measures :   The onely sure method to proceed by was the known *Integrity* and *Prudence* of a *Tutour*, who would improve him if he were regular, if not would certainly tell me it.   Such an one he told me he knew, and would write unto.

Now, full of Instruction, I was not long in getting on Horse-back, but an *unhappy accident* at *Oxford* had almost spoil'd all : for at ten of the Clock in the Inn there was such a roar-
ing

ing and singing that my hair stood an end, and my former Prejudices were so heightned that I resolved to lose the Journey and carry back my Son again, presuming that no noise in *Oxford* could be made but *Scholars* must doe it: But the Proctour coming thither and sending two young pert Townsmen to the Prison for the Riot, relieved my fears, and quickly came to my Chamber, and perceiving my Boy designed for a Gown, told me that it was for the preservation of such *fine Youths* as he that the Proctours made so bold with Gentlemens *Lodgings.* He was a man of Presence and sutable Address, and upon my request sate down; I told him I was glad to see Authority *discountenance* the publick Houses, because it is an incredible *scandal* the University labours under from the account that Countrey Gentlemen (who come and lodge in *Oxford*) give of ranting in Inns and Taverns, as if there was no sleeping in that Town for Scholars: he civily replied, that things might *be better*, but he thanked God they were *no worse;* that Scholars did often bear the blame of *Countrey Gentlemen* and the *Townsmens* guilt, and that absolutely to keep young men from publick Houses was impossible but by *Parents* injunction to their Children, by *Tutours* observing the Conversation of their Pupils, and every Head of an House commanding home in time all the *junior* part at least of their Societies.

As

As for the *Prejudices* we suffer under in the Countrey, he said there were many reasons of that : The constant *Declamations* against us of those intruding Members who were turned out again in 60, the *Hatred* all enemies of King and Church shew against us for being presumed Parties, and the *Envy* the Gentry bear us upon a false supposition of our *Ease, Luxury* and *Prosperity :* to which we our selves (said he) do foolishly contribute by treating Friends in our Chambers as splendidly as if we were worth *thousands,* when perhaps half a Fellowship would not pay for two such *Dinners* as are made upon a slight occasion. And of all men living the *Gentry* ought not to be against us or envy our *moderate* fortunes, whose whole Employment is taken up in serving them, by *breeding* their Sons here, and *serving* their Cures hereafter. Perhaps it will be said the Sons of some of them miscarry : it is great *pity* any one should ; but I am sure that Person ought to vindicate us whose Son goes off *vertuously bred :* they do not know the *care* is taken to secure their Children, and make them happy. I could willingly have heard him longer but that he was to go his *Rounds :* it was pleasant to see how my Son trembled to see the Proctour come in without knocking at his Father's Chamber door.

The next morning I carried my Neighbour's Letter to the *Tutour*, who express'd a
just

just deference to the hand, but did not seem *fond* of the Employment. I thought to have found him mightily *pleased* with the opinion we had of his Conduct, and the credit of having a Gentleman's Son under his charge, and the Father with his Cap in hand: Instead of all this he talked at a rate as if the Gentry were *obliged* to Tutours more than Tutours to them. And when I asked him whether he thought me a man who did not know how to be *gratefull?* No, said he, (with somewhat of sharpness) I never met with a Gentleman backward in that in my life; and to tell you a great Truth, if I were of a *craving Temper*, I would not take half the care I do. For many Mothers (I would say Fathers too were it not for shame) are so wise as to think that man much more accomplished for a Tutour, who can cringe solemnly, tattle in their way, lead them handsomely over a Gutter, and kiss their hands with a good grace, than a man of less *Fashion* and *Ceremony*, who instead of flattering Parents and humouring the Son, sets carefully to work, and lets the Youth know what he comes up for. Though in the mean time I do not think *Clownishness* a Vertue, but *plain Dealing* was always thought so: And some Parents have not wit enough to distinguish these two, especially when they are a little proudish: As for *Ingratitude* in Gentlemen, I never had any reason to complain,

plain, nay I have often refused Presents when I thought my pains over-valued, though I believe (*generally*) an honest Tutour sells his hours cheaper than the Fencer or Dancing-master will. That which I value is the great success and satisfaction I have had in the towardliness and proficiency of a great many young Gentlemen who at this day doe the University *Credit,* and the places where they live *Good,* by their excellent Example: But to be in earnest, the *Care* is infinite, and the Fear they should miscarry is very *Afflicting:* And yet after all this, if the Divine you came from told you that he thought I would undertake your Son for his sake, then I must doe it; and your Son shall know before your own face what he must *trust* to. I do not see any lines of *disobedience* in his Countenance. But I must desire you to lay your *Commands* upon him.

1. That he observe the Duties of the House for Prayers, Exercise, &c. as if he were the Son of a *Beggar:* for when a young Boy is plumed up with a *new Suit,* he is apt to fansie himself a fine thing: Because he hath a peny Commons more than the rest, therefore he ought to be abated a peny-worth of Duty, Learning and Wisedom. Whereas the Gentlemen in the University ought to doe *more Exercise* than others, for they stay but little time there, and ought to be

be accomplish'd in *haste*, because their Quality and the National Concern make them men *apace*. And truly if men may be heard in their own cause, the Gentry are too severe in condemning the Universities for not sending home their Sons furnish'd with *Ethicks, Politicks, Rhetorick, History*, the necessary Learning of a Gentleman, *Logick* and *Philosophy*, &c. and other *usefull Parts ;* when they send up their Sons for two, perhaps three years onely, and suffer them to trifle away half that time too : It is an ungratefull task to the Tutour always to be *chiding*, the Father must command *greater strictness;* otherwise, when the young man who hath been long in *Durance* and here finds his shackles knocked off, and the Gate wide open, he will *ramble* everlastingly, and make it work more than enough for us to keep him sober : whereas if they will take care that he be furnish'd *early* at School with Latin, come up hither young and *pliable*, stay here and study hard for *five years*, then if he prove not able to doe the King and his Countrey service, I am content it should be *our Fault.*

2. That he writes no Letter to come home for the first *whole year.* It is a common and a very great inconvenience, that

soon

soon after a young Gentleman is settled, and but *beginning to begin* to study; we have a tedious ill spell'd Letter from a dear Sister, who languishes and longs to see him as much almost as she doth for a Husband: and this, together with rising to Prayers at six a Clock in the morning, softens the lazy Youth into a fond desire of seeing them too: Then all on the sudden up *Posts* the Livery-man and the led Horse, enquires for the College where the young *Squire* lives, finds my young Master with his Boots and Spurs on *before-hand,* quarrelling the poor man for not coming sooner. The next news of him is at home, within a day or two he is invited to a *hunting match,* and the sickly Youth, who was scarce able to rise to Prayers, can now rise at four of the Clock to a Fox-chase, then must he be treated at an Ale-house with a Rump of Beef seven miles from home, hear an Uncle, Cousin, or Neighbour rant and swear; and after such a sort of *Education* for six or eight weeks, full of tears and melancholy, the sad Soul returns to *Oxford:* his Brains have been so *shogged,* he cannot think in a fortnight: and after all this, if the young man prove debauch'd, the University must be blam'd. And, Sir, if you can bear a Truth I hope you are

not

not concerned in, the first question the Tutour should ask is, In what kind of *Family* and in *what manner* the Child hath been bred up before he comes to us. For where Parents give good Examples themselves, and keep good Order in a Family, the *University Business* is half done to our hands : But if he shall come out of a *Sty* or a *Den*, see his own Father carried up three times a week to Bed ; hear nothing but Oaths and ill language from Servants, *&c.* it must needs vitiate the Virgin Soul, he comes up diseased, and it will require very skilfull application to correct an errour in that first *concoction.*

3. That he frequent not *publick Places*, such as are Bowling Green, Racket Court, *&c.* for beside the danger of firing his bloud by a *Fever*, heightning Passion into *cursing* and *swearing*, he must unavoidably grow acquainted with *promiscuous* Company, whether they are or are not *Vertuous*. Nay, were his new acquaintance all very good, and of the strictest House, the certainty of making him idle by receiving and paying *Treats* and *Visits* is dangerous. I have seen two sorts of Liquour, each of them cold when they were *singly touched*, but when they were put together they flamed with such a degree of heat as melted the Glass they were in. Beside this,

this, all young Gentlemen are not sent to the University with the *same design* with your Son; I know a very honest lusty Countrey Gentleman of four or five thousand a year, who sent his Heir to the University merely for *Credit's* sake; and wisely bid him spend what he would (which the Youth dutifully obeyed) required no more of his *Tutour* than to keep him from knocking his head against a Sign-post, and dirting his silken Stockens at nine of the Clock: do you think such a man fit company for your Son whom you design to be Lord Keeper?

4. Be sure that he discharge all Dues *Quarterly,* and not learn to run into debt, this will make him gain credit and buy cheaper. Whatever he saves of your Allowance let it be his own gain, perhaps that may teach him *thrift,* and if I were fit to be your Tutour I would advise you to *double* it: for Prodigality is a little more catching than Niggardliness with *young Gentlemen.* I know a Person in the world who lived with as much credit in *Oxford* as any man, always Genteel in Habit, and where Entertainments were becoming always generous; and yet carried away with him a good sum of money saved out of his Father's *allowance,* and if he would give me leave

E   I would

I would propose him as an *Example* to the Gentry of the University.

5. Whatever Letters of *Complaints* he writes home I desire you to send me a Copy : for ill-natured, untoward Boys, when they find Discipline sit hard upon them, they then will learn to lie, complain and rail against the University, the College and the Tutour, and with a *whining* Letter, make the Mother, *make the Father* believe all that he can invent, when all this while his main design is to leave the University, and go home again to spanning farthings.

6. I understand by one of your Daughters that you have brought him up a *fine Padd* to keep here for his health's sake, now I will tell you the use of an Horse in *Oxford*, and then doe as you think fit. The Horse must be kept at an *Ale-house* or an *Inn*, and he must have leave to go once *every day* to see him eat Oats, because the Master's eye makes him fat : and it will not be *Genteel* to go often to an House and spend nothing ; and then there may be some danger of the Horse growing *resty* if he be not used often, so that you must give him leave to go to *Abingdon* once every week to look out of the Tavern Window, and see the Maids sell Turnips : and in one month or two come home with a surfeit of poison-

poisoned Wine, and save any *farther charges* by dying : and then you will be troubled to send for your Horse again : This was the unhappiness of a delicate Youth, whose great misfortune it was to be worth two thousand a year before he was *one and twenty.*

7. That he go constantly to the *University Church* on Sundays.

Before I came to be a Tutour, curiosity and a natural share of thoughtfulness, made me observe the *Tempers* of the Youth of the University, such as either *necessity* or *accident* had brought me acquainted with : and I found one too common an humour, which from the beginning I did lament, foreseeing even then a very unhappy consequence of it. You should see young Gentlemen mighty forward to hasten to St. *Mary's*, and happy the man who could get the foremost place in the *Gallery:* but if the Preacher who came up did not please either with his *Looks,* his *Voice,* his *Text* or any *Whimsey* else, immediately a great bustling to get out ; neighbours of each side disturbed to make the Gentleman room : (who sometimes drags half a score along with him) especially if he had a *pointed Band,* and a *silk Suit,* and kept a *brace of Geldings.* Well, when they had *fought* their way

out

out into the Streets, they were for *venturing* their fortunes at another Church; but there the Minister was *practical, dull* and *plain*, and being uncertain what to doe, it being not yet *Dinner* time, they resolved to stumble in at one holy threshold more, and what with staring about on the Auditours, talking aloud of, and censuring the Preacher, they made a hard shift to hold out till the little greezy Bells began to Ring to Veal and Mutton, and then by the *modest admonition* of going out put the Minister in mind of being civil to the rest of the Hearers. Coming home they talk as big as Bull Beef of each man they heard : though if you ask the very Text, (alas!) he talked so low they could never remember that.

At last I perceived that this *Ambulatory Roving* carelesness of humour, begat an indifferency of going to *any Church* at all : and so prepared the young Gentry when they should come to be let loose into the wide world to be no great opposers of *Atheism.*

This was unhappily contributed to, by the Disputes concerning the *Sabbath :* some contending for a very *Jewish* observation; Others disproving its *Morality*, both brought contempt upon that day, and accidentally upon *Religion* it self

self: as did also the Levelling Churches with Stables, and making the *Inward Worship* of God oppose the *Outward.*

For whosoever knows the great *Laziness* and *Stupidity* of the Vulgar, need not be told that Religion is kept up by the distinction of the *Lord's-day* from other days; and if the *Plough* were not stopp'd, a long *Sermon* preach'd, and a *Psalm* or two sung, Religion name and thing would quickly be destroyed, and the Countrey Peoples *Hair* and *Nails* would grow as long as *Nebuchadnezzar's* in the fourth of *Daniel.*

Therefore, I pray Sir, command your Son to be true and just to the *Out-side* of Christian Religion, and leave the rest to God's *Grace* upon the Use of means. Let him not hearken to the Whispers of such as would insinuate distastfull Notions of *Ceremonies* and Church-government; for if he once grows *dis-settled* in his mind from the Publick Worship, then he will pickeer out under every hedge, for a *new Religion,* and finding himself disappointed, 'tis odds but in a twelve months time he may magnifie the *Leviathan,* and when he comes to that, if he doth not cut your Throat (provided he can doe it safely) for fear you disinherit him, truly you are beholden to him.

8. Oblige

8. Oblige him to frequency of *writing
   Home :* For coming to the University is
   not like going beyond Sea, where some
   persons learn to forget their *Relations,*
   and would absolutely slight them, were
   it not for a Bill now and then.   Letters
   to and fro are some kind of *guard* upon
   a youth : and it will not onely be an
   honest means of filling up some idle time,
   but will make him better able to write
   an handsome Letter which is no dis-
   paragement to a Gentleman, or to write
   a good Hand, which few doe.   Beside
   all this, he who begins to contemn his
   Relations, to whom he owes all, will
   quickly reckon *Tutouring* a Relation not
   so considerable and regardable as at first
   he was told.   And in a little time *Commands* will look likeTyranny and Usurpation ; and then Tutour, Father and Vice-
   chancellour, will never be able to balance
   the World, the Flesh and the Devil.

9. I would not have him grow in love with
   Cards and *Dice.*   For though at first
   nothing may seem more harmless than
   to cheat a tedious hour or two with the
   loss of a Trifle : Yet by degrees much
   Play will beget *Skill,* and Skill will beget
   Emulation, this will heighten *wagers :*
   Frequent losses will encrease *Passion :*
   Frequent conquests will make him think
   himself a greater *Gamester* than really he
   is :

is: and whenever he goes so far that Passion blinds what Skill he hath, or Opinion makes him bold of what Skill he hath not, then it will be time to send him up to *London*, to help maintain the Wits of the Town.

Amongst whom, if he loseth, it's likely he is *cheated;* if he winns, then he must fight the man he hath *undone:* and so stake 2000 pounds a year against a Silver Sword: If you do permit him to be fond of *gaming* while he is young, and this doth not befall him, indeed it is none of his *Father's* fault.

10. As for your Allowance and moderate pocket money, it must be at your *discretion;* onely I desire that it may go through my hands, at least the whole first year, till I can take some measures of his *discretion.* I would not have him allowed too little, that he may live like a *Gentleman;* and I would not have him allowed too much, lest he should set up for *nothing else.*

11. That he grow intimate with none but such as I shall recommend to his Acquaintance: Necessity, Good-manners and the customary Respect which is usually paid Strangers, will command a friendly *correspondency* with the members of the same College. But it is of very ill consequence, for an unexperienced,
easie-

easie-natur'd Person of Quality (*the better natur'd, the sooner undone*) to make himself fond of every man who shall court a constant Familiarity, with all the Civility of Address and Friendship.

For if he be a man of *great Acquaintance*, so must you. If he be *Idle*, then by frequent Avocations he will by degrees lessen the *Practice* of your Duty, and jest you out of the *Opinion* of it. Then *Prayers* shall be call'd loss of time ; *Disputations*, School-play ; and *Lectures*, Pedantry : Then the Tutour's presence will become frightfull, Advice useless, and Commands provoking.

12. You must leave him wholly to me, for the *method* of his Study and the Books he must reade, and expect an Account from me of his Abilities and Inclinations in order to a Course of life hereafter.

13. And now, last of all, I must ingenuously tell you *both*, that if he observes all these things, and doth it merely out of a Fear of your Displeasure, and not out of a Sense of his Duty to *God* as well as *Man*, (and secretly wish that he had liberty to be as wild as the worst) it will be but a sort of *Eye-service*, a forced Complement of Good-nature, and never come to much.

But if he be a *serious* and *thinking* Youth, vertuously and religiously inclin'd :

clin'd : if able to consider the Performance of his Duty, as a share of that
service God requires for the Talents he
affords : then he will study without
bidding, and say his Prayers when no
man *sees :* and a Voice then from behind
shall bid him go on and *prosper*, and all the
Care and Kindness in the World, I will
promise you, shall be thought *too little*.

It was very Comical to hear the *differing*
apprehensions I and the rest of the Company
had of this Discourse. For the Women
long'd to go and see the *College* and the
Tutour. And when he was gone out of the
Room, I asked how they liked the Person
and his Converse : My *Boy* clung about his
Mother, and cry'd to go Home again; And
she had no more *wit* than to be of the same
mind, she thought him too weakly to undergo so much Hardship as she foresaw was to
be expected. My Daughters (who instead of
Catechism and Lady's-Calling) had been
used to reade nothing but Speeches in
Romances, and hearing nothing of *Love* and
Honour in all the Talk, fell into downright
scolding at him: call'd him the *Merest* Scholar :
and if this were your *Oxford* Breeding, they
had rather he should go to *Constantinople* to
learn Manners : But I, who was *older* and
understood the Language, call'd them all
great Fools, and told them that there was
so much plain, *practicable Truth* in what he
had

had said, that if every Gentleman would *effectually* take such a Course, it were impossible for one Child in Forty to miscarry.

But perceiving by some part of the Discourse that our Children should be *earlier furnished* in the School with Learning, and so come *sooner* to the University than generally they do, before they are too much their own men, and in sight of *one and twenty :* In behalf of a *young Nobleman* of my near Acquaintance whose eldest Son was about *four or five years of Age*, and who was very solicitous to manage his Education to all the best Advantages, I desired him to furnish me with some Instructions, serviceable to that Noble Family, in the prevention of such Inconveniences as I my self had run into.

He told me that he thought a Child might by *twelve years* of Age be furnished with good skill in Latin and some in Greek, and then after *five years* stay in the University be very well prepared for all the Uses of *Travel*, according to the Methods and Directions in the Book of *Education* and *Gentleman's-Calling*, which can never be read over too often by the Gentry. The most easie and common Advice which every man's Experience shews to be most absolutely necessary, he bad me practise as follows.

General Directions for the better Education of a Child of Great Quality.

1. CUre the Mother of the *Disease* called Fondness if you can, otherwise the Child will be bred so *tenderly* as to be good for little. Every *Door* must be shut, and a *Fire* made in the midst of *July*, while my Young Master's *dressing*, so that most times he doth not prove Hardy enough to be Healthy or Wise. Take a curle-headed Boy from the Side of a Beggar (the phlegmatick offspring of Buttermilk and sour Cheese) who runs Bare-headed all day, and snoars all night upon a bagg of Straw. Take and spirit this rational Clod into *Turky;* after a Course of Hardship ; in thirty years time you may meet him at the Head of an hundred thousand men, *matching Politicks* with all the witty and civilized World. Certainly *Gentlemen* are born with better *Bloud, Spirits* and *Parts* than such a *fellow;* but you see what *Discipline* may doe with one, while through too much *Warmth, Laxity* and *softness* of Skin, the very Soul of the other *transpires* and *wastes.*

2. Though I would not have a Child dealt withall *peevishly,* yet it is of very ill consequence always to gratifie him in the unsati-

unsatiable Wantonness of his little
wishes, this naturally tends to the making
him *humoursome* and *self-will'd*, and all
that the Parents get by that Quality
when he grows towards one and twenty
they may put in their Eyes and see
never the worse. Place a Child at the
Table where there are *twenty Dishes,*
He shall reach out his Finger, point
and call for every one, and when he
hath dined (too *long* by an Hour) ask
him if he will have this or that, he
never fails to say, Yes: which is not
worse for his *Health,* than in other
instances for *Morals.*

3. Good Care ought to be taken what
   Diet the Child eats: For though I
   cannot mechanically shew how heavy
   Pudden and Salt, (or which is worse)
   fresh *Beef,* gets in and mixeth with the
   Soul of a Child, yet I dare say, the
   Learned in Physick are able to prove
   that the more of such things you load
   a tender Stomach with, the longer you
   keep him from being a *Poet* or a *Privy-*
   Councellor. I should go nigh to rail at
   Sweet-meats too, but that we have a
   scurvy Proverb of being ill-natur'd if
   you love them not; whether *Wine*
   (which is now frequently given) be
   proper for Children or no, you were
   best

best consult the *Doctour*. Light Meats,
Chicken, Mutton, *&c.* once every day
and spoon-meat are thought most agreeable.

4. The *Exercise* which a Child should use
   is to be considered : I would not have
   his Motions *violent*, but I would have
   him much *stir*, and often fan his Bloud
   with dry and fresh *Air :* I have heard
   of a certain *Great Lady*, Mother of many
   Children, which deserved as much Fondness as any breathing ; but instead of
   riding in a Coach and Glasses up, made
   them walk out a mile or two in a clear,
   sharp, frosty Morning, put their Noses
   and Lipps into such a *Red* and *Blew*
   that would have made half the Mothers
   in *England* think their Children *Dying,*
   but after this I never heard any man
   complain, that it spoil'd either their
   Health, Beauty or their *Wit.* Of all
   Hardships, use the Child to *rise* early.

5. Care must be taken what Company the
   Child keeps.
       I am not yet come to the incon-
   venient mixture of Persons of Quality
   in the *same School* with Tinkers and
   Coblers Children, which perhaps may
   teach them base, dirty Qualities (they
   were never born to) of Lying, Filching,
                                   Rail-

Railing, Swearing, &c. because I have
not yet resolved my self how it can be
avoided : I am onely now speaking of a
Child very young, and bred at Home.

    I have observed that the eldest Sons
of Great Families lose three years at
least. For the common Cry is, that it
is time enough to learn their Books
when they come to be *seven* or *eight*
years old. This might in a degree be
true enough, if in the mean time they
did onely converse with wise and serious
Companions.

    But when they are able to speak and
prate they begin to be exceedingly *acceptable*, and the Dalliance of every Creature
towards them is obliging ; but all this
while, this doth but invite the useless
Tattle of a foolish *Nurse*, a *Foot-boy*, or
a *Kitchin-wench :* and, if his Mastership
is to be pleased with seeing the Stable
and Sitting on an *Horse*, then he is
farther accomplish'd with the ill-bred
Language and Actions of the *out-lying*
Servants also. This I mention, because
I know some Families in which Children
sometimes better beloved than the rest,
or else because there were *no more*,
having had a constant familiarity and
scarce any other converse than with
Parents, and *those*, Persons of Experience and Thought. The Children have
grown

grown apace into *sense* and *reflexion*, and made wiser Persons asham'd of their own *Age*.

But for a Child to be most in the Company of Servants, and so many *Livery-men* always waiting and bareheaded, if it doth not make the *Living-creature* proud, idle, and think himself fit to be a Lord (before the King and Nation doth) truly he is less of kin to *Adam* than I am.

6. Since this Youth of Quality must be bred up at *Home*, my next advice is, to get a grave, experienc'd well-temper'd Person to manage him, by descending to all the little *Observances* his Age and your Exspectation requires : But then I must have leave to tell you, that your *Allowance* must be very considerable, and his Estate will bear it : For no Wise man will play the Fool to *no purpose* : And if you or his Relations shall fansie that common Maxime, *The cheaper the better*, you will meet with men who will serve and please you and the Child at *present*, who perhaps hereafter will reckon himself no great Gainer, when he finds the want of that Accomplishment which his *Quality* and *Parts* deserve, and that his Brains were sold for twenty pounds a year.

It

It is not well enough considered what it costs to be Learned and Wise, both *pains* and *money* : and whereas Scholars are look'd on as *poor* and *mean*, born to serve them who have the luck to be rich ; yet I do not find truly that great Ones part easily with what they come hard by.

I could tell you of a Person in the World worth some thousands yearly, a Man very considerable for Management, Temper, Justice and all the Qualities of a Gentleman, if he had not placed too much wisedom in *thrift*. He had an eldest Son *incomparable* for Parts and Good-nature, and more willing to be made a Wise man than Boys generally are. But the good Father, to save the *charges* of a great School and boarding abroad any where, was resolved to diet him in Wisedom at his own *Table*, with the cheap assistence of a poor Chaplain, who was to bestow upon him all the week as much Wiseness as ten pounds a year and a good stout Dinner is generally worth.

When the young Heir came towards *Age*, I happened to be acquainted with him, and in some degrees of familiarity; and finding very *fine Parts* in the Rubbish of a great deal of *Clownery*, I once dealt with him very *frowardly*, and ask'd him
plain-

plainly, how it came to pass that he was not a *wiser* man ; *Ask my Father, said he.* And when I replied, that his Father was reputed a discreet Man ; Yes, said the young Gentleman, and I thought him so when I was a young *Child.* But now I am grown up, and the World expects some agreeable Conversation with my *Age, Quality* and *Acquaintance,* I appear so *little* in Company, and am sensible how little I appear, that I wish I had either onely been born with Wit enough not to be *begg'd,* or that my Father had valued the Improvement of my Parts at a *Thousand* a year of my Estate.

7. The Tutour, I propose, will doe well by all the Artifice of kindness and easiness to gain *Affection* from the Child. For otherwise by Force and bare Duty he will learn as little from that Tutour, as a *Farmer* doth from the Minister by the Sermon which is *next* preach'd after he hath paid his *Tithes.*

8. Keep the Child as much as possible out of all Company wherein there may be danger of seeing Actions of *Rudeness, Indecency, Debauchery, Infirmity,* especially if they are committed by near *Relations,* Father, Mother, Brother, *&c.* Incredible

F   is

is the *observation* of Children : and, I dare say, they *think* long before we perceive it ; and the Reverence and Regard they have for Relations recommends all Actions to their Imitation with a strong *Prejudice.*

9. By all Arts of kindness prevent *Frowardness* in him, which will turn to a very ill Quality when he *grows up.*

10. When he is able to speak plain, and capable to be taught, let him learn *Sense and words* together : I mean, teach him such Words as signifie some material Sense, either of *Breeding, Morality* or *Religion,* and not idle, useless words, which signifie nothing but the Folly of such as teach them.

11. When you begin with him, do not *clog* him with too much, to make him *loath* or dread it, but let him come to the Book as to his *Recreation,* or to gain *Credit.*

12. Accustome him to kind and friendly words even towards *Servants* and *Inferiours.* This will not onely be obliging but will habituate the Child to Respect and Decency to men of *higher Degree,* to Parents and Tutour himself ; and be sure to instruct him of the *regard* to be had according to mens *different* Qualities.

13. The

13. The method how to teach him *Latin* with most advantage and expedition I must wholly leave to the Tutour : For whether it be sooner learn'd by the *Rules* of Grammar as is done in Schools, or barely by Construing *Authours* and talking Latin with the Child always, by which sometimes Gentlemen are taught, I am not able to answer mine own Arguments for each : Use him much to Translation which I think much better than Composition.

14. Be sure to keep him constant to *Devotion*, and let not his own private prayers be *tedious* and *wearisome*.

15. Make him able to reade *Greek*, and turn the *Lexicon* upon occasion, as far as the Greek *Testament*.

16. A short Series of the History and Chronology of the *Old Testament*, by Question and Answer, with a general Knowledge of the Globes, would be usefull, and make him proud of Learning.

17. The excellent Qualities of *Cyrus* in *Xenophon* translated and commended would be an admirable Pattern for Emulation.

18. Of

18. Of all the good Qualities, from the very beginning, accustome the Child to *speak the Truth*, and when he is faulty, do not affright him into lying, and silly excuses (which Servants commonly teach them) but by mildness and *security* from chiding, at the first beget in him the *courage* of confessing his faults: Great Actions of Honour and Justice depend upon *Veracity*.

19. Whatever the Child doth well, either voluntary or out of observance of former Commands, be sure let him have *Commendation* enough, this is a principal Reward and tickles the proud Flesh.

20. Let no Person chide the Child who is in a great fit of Anger, lest the *violence* of it make him moped, or the *indecency* of it make him grow careless.

21. I would not have Parents or Tutour be *always* chiding for little things : those will better be mended by persuasion; and to chide for *every* fault alike, will in time make the Youth think great faults no worse than little ones, and reproving a mere thing of course ; 'tis the *Common*, but a very inartificial way.

22. Whenever you find the Child in an
Extra-

Extravagant fit of Froppishness and
Anger (how little soever be the provoca-
tion) do not express anger to him at *that
time*, but immediately sweeten him, take
his part, and get him out of the fit as
soon as you can, lest it grow *violent* and
lasting, and at a cooler season argue the
indecorum with him, when *Reason* will
come in to his assistence.

23. Never disgrace the Child or upbraid
him with his Follies before *Strangers :*
this may cut him too much, and never
be forgotten ; and it will be very obliging
when he is afterwards made understand
how kind you were in moderating your
reproofs for his *Honour's* sake.

24. Let not the Child be frighted with
horrid stories of Bug-bears or idle tricks
in the dark : the ill consequences may
be very great.

25. Never let him be accustom'd to laugh
at mens natural *Infirmities*, but give him
occasion from thence of thanking God
who hath made the *Difference*.

26. Magnifie and help him to admire the
glorious parts of the Creation and variety
therein : this will beget early Notions of
Reverence and Honour for the *Maker*.

27. Keep

27. Keep him from hearing any *Paradoxes* disputed in the place where he is, either of Religion, Morality, Government, *&c.* and when ever it happens, let him see his Parents and Tutour undertake always the *better* side.

28. A good short Collection of *Proverbs* out of *Solomon,* and the Proverbs of each single Nation (wherein their Wisedom consists) such as respect *God, Religion, good Manners, civil Breeding* and *Duty* in all Relations, well digested into a Method, and under *proper Heads,* to be judiciously explained to the Child at leisure times, would be of incomparable use : Because that short, grave, sententious way of Instruction sticks better in the *Memory* and helps his *Thinking.*

29. Let him reade nothing by himself which is not very *easie* for him to comprehend, lest it discourage his reading : and let all your Discourses with him be very *plain,* and of such things as he is capable to be instructed in : this will help and *draw out* his Parts, whereas Difficulties will *baulk* and *stifle* them.

30. If you find him begin to grow *pert* and *forward,* never check him, but you must

must be sure to *modifie* his Wit, you
must set limits, and say hitherto and no
farther, bound it with Good-nature and
Decency: For there is one Quality
mightily *taking*, and especially if it discover it self early in a Child, which is
to *Jeer* and *Reflect* upon Men and their
Actions: Beside the Impudence, Ill-
nature, and Abusive Language which
this is generally attended with (and so
is the most unbecoming Breeding for a
Gentleman) it many times proves very
dangerous in *promiscuous* Company. It
is not long since, for a Sentence no
greater than the Wise mens of *Greece*
(and not half so witty) a fine Gentleman
had his Brains beaten out: *Cicero* was
a great *Jester*, but the cry went on
Antony's side for Wit, when he had
gotten his Head off.

31. If you find him impetuously in *love*
with any thing you do not like, you
must not *bluntly* and *suddenly* check him,
this may make him love it the more,
and look on you as the *Enemy* of his
Happiness; but by degrees lessen the
value of the Object, persuade him of its
disagreeableness, and divert him with
something more innocent, and of a
differing nature,
    Alterius vires subtrahit alter amor.
                                    32. If

32. If you find him apt to take *offence* at any single man's Person, disgust and hate him ; by all means strive to qualifie this, never rest till you have made him a Friend, let him know the *Duty* and have the *Honour* of Forgiving. This may be of use if he live to be a *great* Man.

33. If you find him inclining to Thoughtfulness, Sadness and Sighing, correct it with all imaginable pains by pleasant Converse, light Diets, cheerfull Recreations, delightfull Readings, lest he get an Habit, and at last grow *Melancholy*, that is, useless and unserviceable.

34. Take all occasions in *his Company* to magnifie *Vertue* and debase *Vice :* Furnish him with Examples of both out of Scripture, of God's Judgments and Deliverances : but till he is ripe enough to be instructed, you may forbear letting him reade those Chapters wherein the *failings* of good Men are recorded. The Plainness and Spirit of Devotion contained in the *Psalms,* speak them fittest to be read by a Child.

These (said the Tutour to me) are the *uppermost* Rules that occur as *absolutely* necessary to be observed in the first breeding

ing of the Person of Quality you talk of:
Though, if your Dinner did not wait you,
perhaps I might think of more, but first try
these *effectually*, and consult the Book of
Education for other necessary Instructions.

I heartily thanked him, and finding it late,
I invited him to Dinner with me at the *Inn*,
but he refused, saying that such Houses
were not built for *Gown-men*, and made me
leave my Son to dine with him, having (said
he) observed the great *Improvidence* of the
Gentry, who when they come to enter a Son,
(which is commonly at the *Act*, that solemn
season of *Luxury*) bring *Wife* and *Daughters*
to shew them the University; there's mighty
Feasting and drinking for a week, every
Tavern examin'd and all this with the company of a Child, forsooth, sent up hither for
Sobriety and *Industry*.

After this he invited us the next day to a
Commons, and according to his *Humour* before, I expected to have been *starved* in his
Chamber, and the Girles drank Chocolette
at no rate in the morning for fear of the
worst.

It was very pleasant to see, when we came,
the *constrain'd* Artifice of an unaccustomed
Complement, Silver Tankards heaped upon
one another, Napkins some twenty years
younger than the rest, Glasses fit for a
Dutchman at an *East-India Return.*

And at last came an Entertainment big
enough

enough for ten *Members* of the House : I was asham'd, but would not disoblige him, considering with my self that I should put this man to such a charge of forty shillings at least, to entertain me, when for all his honest care and pains he is to have but forty or fifty shillings a Quarter, so that for one whole Quarter he must doe the drudgery to my Son for nothing.

After Dinner I went to the publick *Bowling Green*, it being the onely Recreation I can affect. Coming in, I saw half a score of the finest Youths the Sun, I think, ever shined upon : they walked to and fro, with their hands in their Pockets, to see a match played by some Scholars and some Gentlemen fam'd for their skill. I gaped also and stared as a man in his way would doe : But a Country ruff Gentleman, being like to *lose*, did swear at such a rate that my heart did grieve that those fine young men should *hear* it, and know there was such a thing as *swearing* in the Kingdom. Coming to my Lodging, I charged my Son never to go to such publick places unless he resolved to quarrel me.

Having *settled* my Son and left my commands with him we all made haste home again, in earnest much better satisfied with the *Government* of the University than I was before : for all this while I had as critically observed all miscarriages as a *prejudiced* man may be imagined to doe.

And

And (to say more) when we were summon'd thither a while before to sit in *Parliament*, I was resolved narrowly to scan the carriage of the University towards the *Members*, to understand the temper and opinion, as far as the free converse in *Coffee Houses* (where every man's *Religion* and *Politicks* are quickly seen) could discover.

The plainness and freedom *young Masters* us'd was odd at the first, but afterwards very pleasant, when it appeared to be a kind of *Trade* not Policy : For being used all the week long to dispute Paradoxes, the Disputacity reached afterwards to matter of *Religion* and *State*. But in fine I perceived there was nothing of design or malice in all this, but a *road* of Converse, arising partly out of hatred to *Fanaticks* and want of *experience* and conversation in the world, which teaches men to be more cautious in promiscuous discourse.

As for their *Civility* to the Members we must own it, we had their Lodgings (as good as they were) for nothing, with civility and respect whereever they met us *agreeable :* when at the same time the *Townsmen* put Dutch rates upon their Houses that under five or six pound a week a Whig could not have ,*room enough* to speak Treason in. I could not perceive but they both talked and preached against Popery as much as any men, though in the business of Succession
they

they still favoured the Duke.   I walk'd the
Streets as late as most people, and never in
ten days time ever saw any Scholar rude or
disordered : so that as I grow old, and more
engaged to speak the *truth*, I do repent of
the *ill opinion* I have had of that place, and
hope to be farther obliged by a very good
account of my Son.

And upon the whole matter let me offer
you one *Caution*, when you cry out *Idle*,
Ignorant, Ill-bred, Debauch'd, Popish University, I am sure you speak at a venture, and
do but echo the *ill-natured* Fame of things :
And ill Language doth not become the
mouth of a *Gentleman* though the matter be
true.   But I am now convinced that we
wrong them; As for their Idleness, the
Graver sort kept close : 'tis true Curiosity
brought out the *young* Gentlemen to see new
Faces and shew their new Ribbons: for
Ignorance we are not Judges, and the Nation
generally frees them from that : for their
Ill-breeding, Simplicity and Plainness is their
Guise, and they look upon all things else as
Art.   *Debauchery* may happen among some
of so many, but all my Acquaintance abomi-
nate it as much as you and I do.   And as
for *Popery*, the most serious men I knew
there study to make themselves able to resist
the *Temptation :* so that for us of the Gentry
to rail at them for *Popishly* affected, and
men

men forlorn as to Protestant Religion, is very *Unjust* and *Uncharitable.*

In the *next place* you beg my direction in the *management of the Canvas:* I confess I shall never be able to admire enough the most excellent Constitution of our Government by way of a Parliament, wherein the meanest Subject hath his just regard, and forty shillings a year makes a man wise enough to chuse his *Representative:* nay now of late very *Cottagers* and *Quakers* come in for a share in electing that Assembly, which for ought I know turns and winds the great Affairs of all *Europe:* Though I must confess I am sorry, that in *Elections* so little regard is had to the Wisedom and Vertue of the Candidate, and that so much use is made of the *Ignorance* and *Vices* of the people.

It will not be safe to depend upon the vulgar of your own Party, because many of them will appear to have no Votes either on Account of *Swearing* or *Estates;* and yet their Zeal for the Cause will hurry them on to poll.

If you manage your self wisely, I know no man can make a better *Figure* in the Field than you, and thus, presuming of you in the *House,* I will next give you my thoughts concerning your *Behaviour* there. For the least misbehaviour at *first coming* is not easily forgotten in that Place.

1. I will

1. I will recommend and furnish you with Books and Copies which give an Account of the Original, Privileges and Proceedings in that House, which will make you capable to act very serviceably, whether you prove a great Speaker or no.

2. It will be the best use you can make of the first three or four months (if you sit so long) to be particularly acquainted with the Face, Parts and Designs of every Member, more particularly, I advise you,

    1. Not to be a Speaker *too soon,* which is incident to Youth.

    2. Whenever you speak, your native *Modesty* will be very becoming, and *Brevity* withall ; for we old Stagers did always look on it as our Privilege to be *tedious.*

    3. Meddle with no man's *Person,* because you do not know how many you disoblige ; do not begin early to reply to other mens Speeches, because such a man ought to be very considering and ready.

    4. Never speech it when you are provoked to

to be *angry*, because it will be hard then to act with *decency*, required in so great a Meeting.

5. Study not to be much *concern'd* when you are replied upon with Sharpness or Jeer.

6. Beware of discovering any Affectation of being *Witty :* for that shews you pleased with what you say, which is unacceptable, and beneath the Opinion you ought to have of an Assembly so august. Do not affect great Words, for a design to be thought Learned shews the *want ;* and the more knowing any man is, the *plainer* he is able to express his mind. But, on the other side, you must not descend to low and mean expressions, that will savour of an *ungenteel* Breeding. Beware of all unusual motions and gestures of Head, Eyes, Hand, Body, or the like.

7. When any matter of great moment is debated, be not *forward* to speak, because at your Age it is impossible you should comprehend the matter, design and managery of the Case. But be sure at such a time to *frequent* the House, and be a diligent Auditour
for

for then you will hear the *Reason, Law, Policy* and *Eloquence* of our English Gentry: Masculine Eloquence which flows upon all Occasions, not constrain'd to the fulsome *Anaphora's* and *Paranomasia's* of the modern Rhetoricians, those Whistles and Rattles of *Schoolboys:* Not but those Figures when they were first, or now when they are wisely used, are good Ornaments: But it is a vast mistake to transplant those Flowers out of the fertile soil of *Cicero* and the Ancients, and think they will thrive and grow in every *Clodpate;* to think that those Schemes in a small Epitome, robb'd of the Advantages to be understood, such as are the *Occasion, Person, Time, Connexion,* &c. should by being barely learn'd by heart, make every Puny able to imitate the *greatest Master* of Speech in all mankind.

When you come once to be taken notice of; then remember to fortifie your self against solicitations to serve a *Party,* and that from men who will think they doe you *Honour* to vouchsafe you a gratious *Nod:* the Inconveniences will be many.

1. Under *Pretence* of preparing Business
you

you must be a Slave to Clubbs of twelve, one, two, three of the Clock, whereby the Health will be impaired and ill Habits gotten.

2. You must then resolve to *captivate* your Judgment to the Opinion of the Leading-men of your Party. And then your own Reason will be quite lost, you will never attempt to examine the true merit of the Cause, and so many times be betray'd to the eager persuit of what you would abhor did you well consider what perhaps your mighty Leader pursues out of *Passion, Interest* or Human *Inadvertency,* when all the while you think he doth act with due *Deliberation, Integrity* of *Intention,* and merely on *Publick good :* such an Authoritative Leading-man is the Bane of any *Society* whatever.

3. You must expect to bear a share in Answering for all the *Imprudences* of your Party. No number was ever so happily combined, but that some Persons in it would be apt to act some *extravagant* Part, out of Zeal to serve a Cause, which will make a Thinking-man blush to favour.

4. You certainly create Enemies to your
G self

self, all of the *opposite* Persuasions, though you never had thoughts or design so to doe. All Acts of unkindness received, or Acts of Revenge threatned, shall respect you as one of the Party, who are purely simple and passive, as much as if you had been the *first* Mover or Executioner of the whole ; this makes *Neighbours, Friends, Kindred,* at Daggers drawing when e'er they meet : Believe it, the necessary *Mixture* and Complication of your Affairs in the World, and the *various Relations* you must bear, will afford you Contrasting more than enough. Create as few Troubles to your self as you can.

An

An INDEX of the most remarkable *Common-Places* hinted in the foregoing Papers.

The

AN INDEX.

F I N I S.

THE COUNSELS

OF

WILLIAM DE BRITAINE.

A VOLUME OF SEVENTEENTH-CENTURY PRECEPTS AND APHORISMS,

REVISED BY

HERBERT STURMER,

Author of " Some Poitevin Protestants in London."

SOME PRESS NOTICES.

" Mr. Sturmer has accomplished his 'toil' well and carefully; his introduction is excellent. . . . The author, whoever he was, knows how to turn an aphorism with so neat a touch that he must have been ancestor of Mr. George Meredith."—*Pall Mall Gazette.*

" 'The Counsels of William de Britaine' are full of wit and wisdom throughout, and may be read to-day with direct profit to many. Mr. Sturmer is to be thanked for re-introducing them to the world."—*National Observer and British Review.*

" By no means unfit to be ranked with Gracian and Osborne."—*Manchester Guardian.*

" A work of considerable interest."—*Glasgow Herald.*

" There are many nuggets in the 'Counsels' for those who know gold when they see it."—*Manchester Courier.*

" Whatever his subject, he treats it 'wittily,' and the various essays abound in anecdotes and epigrams, so that, open the book where you will, you are sure to find some good thing confronting you."—*Sheffield Telegraph.*

" The 'Counsels' are divided into thirty-two sections dealing with as many subjects, in a pithy and proverbial fashion. Mr. Sturmer's work of revision must have been exceedingly difficult, and, so far as we can judge, it has been excellently done."—*The Guardian.*

" It is certainly one of those volumes which, having once read, one dislikes to see absent from one's shelf."—*Cape Times.*

" It is full of wise saws and modern instances."—*Daily News.*

" Each of the thirty-two sections abounds in wholesome advice, clever aphorisms, and suggestive illustrations. There is scarcely a page that does not lend itself to quotation."—*Antiquary.*

" The wit and wisdom of the author is no less to be admired than his depth of learning and his wide knowledge of the ancient classics."—*Church Bells.*

" . . . Is not unworthy of a place beside the essays of Bacon."—*Christian World.*

LONDON :

F. E. ROBINSON, 20, GREAT RUSSELL STREET, BLOOMSBURY.

𝕬niBersities of Oxford & CamBridge.

Two Series of Popular Histories of the Colleges.

Mr. F. E. Robinson, M.A., Cantab., has much pleasure in announcing that he is about to publish two series of Oxford and Cambridge College Histories. The Oxford Series will consist of twenty-one and the Cambridge Series of eighteen volumes.

Each volume will be written by someone officially connected with the College of which it treats, or at least by some member of that College who is specially qualified for the task. It will contain (i.) a history of the College from its foundation; (ii.) an account and history of its buildings; (iii.) notices of the connection of the College with any important social or religious events; (iv.) a list of the chief benefactions made to the College; (v.) some particulars of the contents of the College library; (vi.) an account of the College plate, windows and other accessories; (vii.) a chapter upon the best known and other notable but less well-known members of the College.

Each volume will be produced in crown octavo, in a good clear type, and will contain about 200 pages (except two or three volumes which will be thicker). The illustrations will consist of full-page plates containing reproductions of old views of the Colleges and modern views of the buildings, grounds, etc.

The two Series will extend over a period of about two years, and no particular order will be observed in the publication of the volumes. It is hoped that the first volume will be ready in January next.

Price 5s. net per volume.

The writers' names are given on the opposite page.

F. E. ROBINSON,
20, Great Russell Street,
London, W.C.

November, 1897.

Oxford Series.

COLLEGE.			
University	...	...	A. C. Hamilton, M.A.
Balliol	...	...	H. W. Carless Davis, B.A.
Merton	...	...	B. W. Henderson, B.A.
Exeter	...	...	W. K. Stride, M.A.
Oriel	...	...	D. W. Rannie, M.A.
Queen's	...	...	Rev. J. R. Magrath, D.D.
New	...	...	Rev. Hastings Rashdall, M.A.
Lincoln	...	...	Rev. Andrew Clark, M.A.
All Souls	...	...	C. Grant Robertson, M.A.
Magdalen	...	...	Rev. H. A. Wilson, M.A.
Brasenose	...	...	J. Buchan.
Corpus Christi	...	...	Rev. T. Fowler, D.D.
Christ Church	...	...	Rev. H. L. Thompson, M.A.
Trinity	...	...	Rev. H. E. D. Blakiston, M.A.
St. John's	...	...	Rev. W. H. Hutton, B.D.
Jesus	...	...	E. G. Hardy, M.A.
Wadham	...	...	J. Wells, M.A.
Pembroke	...	...	Rev. Douglas Macleane, M.A.
Worcester	...	...	Rev. C. H. O. Daniel, M.A.
Hertford	...	...	S. G. Hamilton, M.A.
Keble	...	...	D. J. Medley, M.A.

Cambridge Series.

Peterhouse	...	...	Rev. T. A. Walker, LL.D.
Clare	...	...	J. R. Wardale, M.A.
Pembroke	...	...	W. S. Hadley, M.A.
Caius	...	...	J. Venn, Sc.D., F.R.S.
Trinity Hall	...	...	H. T. Trevor Jones, M.A.
Corpus Christi	...	...	Rev. H. P. Stokes, LL.D.
King's	...	...	Rev. A. Austen Leigh, M.A.
Queens'	...	...	Rev. J. H. Gray, M.A.
St. Catharine's	...	...	The Lord Bishop of Bristol.
Jesus	...	...	A. Gray, M.A.
Christ's	...	...	J. Peile, Litt.D.
St. John's	...	..	J. Bass Mullinger, M.A.
Magdalene	...	...	W. A. Gill, M.A.
Trinity	...	...	Rev. A. H. F. Boughey, M.A., and J. Willis Clark, M.A.
Emmanuel	...	...	E. S. Shuckburgh, M.A.
Sidney	...	...	G. M. Edwards, M.A.
Downing	...	...	Rev. H. W. Pettit Stevens, M.A.
Selwyn	...	...	Rev. A. L. Brown, M.A.

SELECTIONS FROM THE

BRITISH SATIRISTS,

With an Introductory Essay by

CECIL HEADLAM,

Late Demy of Magdalen College, Oxford.

Crown 8vo., pp. 330, cloth gilt, 6s.

[READY

THE

GUARDIAN'S INSTRUCTION,

OR

THE GENTLEMAN'S ROMANCE.

Written for the diversion and service of the Gentry.

This quaint little book contains a defence of the University of Oxford, interesting details of life at Oxford, and advice to parents of position on the education of their sons.

Reprinted from the edition of 1688. *With a Biographical Introduction.*

Fcap. 8vo., pp. 120, cloth gilt, 2s. 6d.

LONDON :

F. E. ROBINSON, 20, GREAT RUSSELL STREET, BLOOMSBURY.